Dedication

This book is dedicated to Master Yuan Chu Cai.
The original author of "Iron Palm"

Iron Power Palm

By Gareth Thomas

Published by:

IronPowerPalm.com
Unit 12 / 30 upper Queen Street
Auckland, New Zealand
1010

All Rights Reserved. No part of this book may be reproduced or transmitted in any form or by any means, electronic or mechanical, including photocopying, recording or by any information storage and retrieval system without written permission of the author except for use in brief quotations in a book review.

Copyright © 2011 by IronPowerPalm.com
First Edition 2011
ISBN 978-0-473-18221-2
Published in New Zealand

Disclaimer

Anyone who undertakes the practices as outlined in this book does so at his or her own risk. The information in this book is meant to supplement, not replace, proper exercise training. All forms of exercise pose some inherent risks. The author advises readers to take full responsibility for their safety and know their limits. The exercise, dietary programs and herbal recipes in this book are not intended as a substitute for any exercise routine, medical treatment or dietary regimen that may have been prescribed by your doctor. As with all exercise and dietary programs, you should get your doctor's approval before beginning. Every effort has been made to ensure that the Chinese terms used in this book have been translated accurately. Should there be any omissions or errors in this respect we apologize and shall be pleased to make corrections where applicable in any future edition.

Iron Power Palm

Iron Power Palm

by

Gareth Thomas
www.IronPowerPalm.com

Contents

Introduction 9
Preface 11
   Iron Palm In 97 Days 11
      The origin of the Iron Palm 12
      The Formal Exercises (Chuan) in relation to the Basic Exercises (Kung) 13
      Age and Iron Palm Training 14
      Training in the Basic Exercises (Kung) in relation to Medication 15
      The three important requisites in training 15
      The different schools and their methods 17
   The 97 day method 18
      Equipment: 18
      Method 19
      Medication 26
      Precautions 26
      Other measure: 27
      Testing out 27
   Internal training methods 29
      The "All Round" method itself 31
      Pushing Mountains 34
      Plucking Stars 36
      Lifting The Sky 39
      The Chi must emanate from the Tan Tien 41
      "Strength must permeate to the hollow of the palm." 42
   Methods of Ancient Chinese Gong 42
      Bamboo Leaf Hand 42
      Sand Bag Training 44
      Iron Arm 46
      Iron Hand 50
      Tornado Palm 50
      Finger Gong Methods (One Finger Zen) 51
   Ancient Chinese Bodybuilding and Strength Gong 52
      Weight Vest Training 52
      Wrist Roller 54
      Sluice Gate 54
      Kettle Bell Training 55
      Hand Strengthening 56

Section One: Iron Palm By Yuan Chu Cai 61

Chapter 1: The Division of Inner Gong and Outer Gong. 65
   Section 1: Inner Qi Gong 66
   Section 2: External Qi Gong 69
      (1) Punching the sandbag (Bamboo Leaf Hand) 69
      (2) Hitting the Wooden Dummy 71
      (3) Rolling sand tube 72

Chapter 2: Outer Qi Gong 75
   Section 1 Massage/Beating 75
      (a) Massage and beating 75
      (b) Beating 75
   Section 2: Method of Medicine Manufacture 76
      1. Method of Making Pills 76

Chapter 3: Gymnastic Qi Gong 79
   Section 1: Walking on the Wall 79
   Section 2: Walking on the Tight Rope 80
   Section 3: Walking on Wooden Piles 80

Chapter 4: Iron Palm (Jabbing) 83
   Section 1: Fingers 83
      1. Parallel Stance Downward Finger Stabbing 83
      2. Left Hand Crouching Stance inclined Finger Stabbing 84
      3. Right 85
      4. Grabbing Method 86
      (1) Double Thrust with Bow stance 88
      (2) Right Thrust with Hook-Step 89
      (3) Left Thrust with Side-Step 90

Chapter 5: Iron Palm (Slapping) 93
   Section 2: Palm 93
      (1) Parallel stance slap 93
      (2) Leftward Palm with Bow-Step 94
      (3) Rightward Palm with Hook-Step 95
      (1) Horse stance Striking palm 96
      (2) Horse Stance Right Palm Back Hook 97
      (3) Left hand Reversed Palm with Hook-Step 98
   Right Hand reversed Palm... 99
   Knife Hand Bow Step.. 100
   Section 3: Hand and Fist 101
      1. Side Fist with parallel feet 101
      2. Thrust Fist with Hook-step 104

Chapter 6: Elbow 107
   Section 4: Elbow 107
      1. Sandbag Method 107
      2. Arm Roller 110

Five Feng and Six Elbows 117
   Section 1: Method of the Five Feng 117
      (1) Head Feng (use at your own discretion) 117
      (2) Head (back/side) feng 118
      (3) Shoulder Feng 119
      (4) Hip Feng 120
      (5) Knee Feng 121
   Section 2: Method of the Six Elbows 123
      (1) Sitting Elbow 123
      (2) Side Elbow 124
      (3) Heart Elbow 126
      (4) Lifting Elbow 127
      (5) Pressing Elbow 129
      (6) Binding Elbow 130

Iron Palm Secrets 133
   1. What is it? 133
   2. Training 141
   3. Chi 149
   4. Equipment 150
   5. Dit Da Jow 152
   6. Additional Questions 168

Part 3: Hand & Forearm Strength for Martial Artists 175
   Introduction 175
   Training Principles 176
   Intensity Training 176
   Volume Training 179
   Progressive Resistance 180
   Negative Reps 182
   Forced Reps 183
   Periodization 183
   Types Of Hand Strength 184
   Anatomy of the Hand 185
   Equipment 187
      Hand Grippers 187
      Thumb Clamps (Spring Clamp) 195
      Eagle Catcher 196
      Gripinator 197
      Ivanko Gripper 198

- Wrist Roller 202
- Sledge Hammer 202
- Manila Rope 203
- Telegraph Tapper 204
- Elastic Bands 205
- Thomas Inch Dumbell (Thick Bar Training) 206
- Pinch Grips (Block / Blob) 208
- Gyroscope Balls 209
- Chinese Balls (Baodang Balls) 210

Grip Exercises 211
- Hand Gripper 211

Common Barbell & Dumbell Exercises 215
- Pinch Grip 215
- Hammer Curl 219
- Wrist Curl 223
- Training Tips & Secrets 228
- Preacher Wrist Curl 228
- Reverse Barbell preacher Curl 232
- Variations 236
- Reverse Wrist Curl 237
- Zottman Curl 241
- Reverse Barbell Curl 244
- Wrist Roller 249
- Reverse Dumbbell Curls 252
- Variations 255
- Reverse Cable Curl 256
- Dead lift 258

Additional Training 260
Tui Na Hand and Arm Massage 261
- Arm & Hand Massage 263
- Tennis Elbow Treatment 271
- Carpal Tunnel Treatment 272
- Remedial exercises: 274

Sample Routines For Iron QiGong & Strength Training 276

Resources 283
- Iron Palm: 283
- Grip Strength Training: 284

After word 285

INTRODUCTION

THIS book will introduce you to an extensive program for training your Iron Palm and developing the conditioning requisite to breaking bricks and concrete.

After a year of this training you will be ready to learn the actual fighting skill to apply this conditioning. In this manual we keep to the conditioning only.

As an introduction I have decided to include selected excerpts from "Iron Palm in 100 Days" and to outline some additional forms of Chinese Gong that you can use in your personal program. Many of these additional methods come from the 72 Shaolin methods but there are other sources included also.

A message about realistic expectations, Iron Palm requires a minimum commitment of 30 minutes per day plus warm up and massage. This is for the training of hands only. If you decide to train Iron Arm also this will require another 30 minutes per day. Iron Body will require yet another 30 minutes plus massage and meditations. So this is a commitment of two to three hours daily to Qi Gong. On top of this 3-4, forty-five minute weight training sessions should be done per week, a daily stretching routine and daily cardio with a jump rope or kettlebell.

So you see there is a great deal of dedication and time involved in becoming a master of Qi Gong Martial Arts. The reward is remarkable ability.

Preface

Iron Palm In 97 Days

EXPERTS in the art of Iron Palm have existed in China for many hundreds of years. Some of them attained unimaginable skill in this art.

The school of inner pugilism is accepted to have started during the Ming Dynasty (1368 - 1662). Since this time the art of Iron Palm was degraded and neglected by students and mentors as an unworthy art. For this reason the great art fell into oblivion and was taken up by vagrants and charlatans.

The Iron Palm is a killing art and a military skill. The ability to break bricks, stone and concrete means little without the skill and temperance to apply it correctly in combat. As a killing art it may contravene your moral code of ethics. If that is the case you can choose not to follow this path. For those with the self discipline to learn Iron Palm and control the power it imparts without moral dilemma there are healing benefits from the conditioning in the form of enhanced chi in the hands. Just as One Finger Zen is both a fighting and healing art so too is Iron Palm.

In recent years, Chinese Martial Arts have gained great popularity in the west and many great secrets have been revealed in China and to the world. Martial Arts of Japan, Korea and many other nations have equally become popular so the peril of improper training and damage to the hands is more common place. Many practise using the "Direct Method" which uses no medication and relies upon disfigurement of the hand as adaptation. Thus, injury of the hand bones and disfigurement of the hands, are not uncommon occurrences. In the hope that future enthusiasts can avoid such unnecessary mishaps the author proposes therefore to write this book and to disclose the innermost secrets in training. He ascertains that if the instructions here are carried out to the very letter, mastery of the Iron Palm can be achieved three months. It must be remembered however that Iron Palm is a killing art and the author strongly advises it's use only in moments of absolute necessity. Its indiscriminate use and its use to bully others, is strongly deprecated. Always remember that a skilful person will always meet with another yet more skilful. Also, the laws of a country and the laws of Nature make killing a criminal offence and a mortal sin. Those who, therefore apply their skill wrongfully, invite their own doom.

Be at peace within your self and acquire emotional discipline so as not to apply the Iron Palm in anger, malice or vanity.

The origin of the Iron Palm

Throughout the past 1000 years there have been many experts in the art of Iron Palm, but it is unknown from what dynasty or person this skill originated from. The Shaolin texts are the oldest record, "Yi Chin Ching or Sinew Changing" has a detailed account of Iron Palm training. Today in the 21st century the ancient Shaolin methods are no longer secret. The first recorded methods are a hard external style of training as follows...

After basic training, energy is reserved for training the hand. The method is to wash the hands in luke warm water and then gradually wash them in water that is boiling hot. The whole palm and the wrist must be immersed in such water. After withdrawing the hands from the immersion and without any attempt to wipe them dry, they are waved about, while at the same time, a conscious effort is made by the mind to have the 'Chl' traverse across the hand towards the finger tips. As to strengthening the fingers, the method used is to mix both black and green peas in a container and to thrust the hand into these peas repeatedly. The first method described is the "Washing method" which is designed to improve the circulation and the second method using peas, is designed to harden the skin through friction.

Training in the manner described, will in time, allow Chi to reach the finger tips giving them power and strength. At the same time the skin, ligaments and bones, will be hardened. When not in use, such seasoned hands, would not differ from those of a normal person but, when called to action, they are as hard as iron and nothing can withstand them. This is because strength emanates, from the bones. After going through this section of the Shaolin text, it can be surmised that the Iron Palm probably owes it's origin to this source.

The Formal Exercises (Chuan) in relation to the Basic Exercises (Kung)

The formal exercises are the techniques and forms of the Martial Art. To train only in these methods is rather pointless. The basic exercises provide the foundation of conditioning. The foundation is a prerequisite to the formal training. Without "Kung", form training is weak and lacking in strength and power. That is why famous masters of the past, as well as those of the present, never bias themselves by concentrating only on one aspect of a dualistic art.

The basic exercises, can be classified into the external and internal type. Generally that which can be seen is "external" and that which can not is "internal". The internal type aims at training the Chi. The sitting meditative method of the Shaolin School and the "Guiding" method of the Wu Tang School belong to this category. The internal type is difficult to master without the assistance of a good teacher but today we have electronic technology which can assist by showing us aspects of our physiology that were invisible in the past. The external type aims at toughening the bones, ligaments and skin. The Iron Palm, the Iron Vest belong to this category. This latter category, is also quite remarkable in that by training in it, one can reach such a state of perfection, that the skin, muscles and bones would be so hardened that even swords and lances could not pierce them.

The external type again can be subdivided into the hard and soft type. In comparison, the soft type is more difficult to master for after acquisition of the art, internal injury can be inflicted on an opponent, without any obvious sign of external injury. Further a stage could be arrived at, when a punch can be delivered, to cause the death of another without direct physical contact, to be able to perfect the art to this stage is akin to mastery of the internal type mentioned above. The "Cinnabar palm" and the "Light weighted art" belong to this variety.

The hard type in comparison with the soft, is easier to master. It aims at external strength yet, it's effects can be frightening. If there is perseverance, it can be mastered even without the assistance of a teacher provided that certain recommended measures are followed. Because of it's easiness, many take up this type of training. The Iron Forearm and the Angel's Palm belong to this variety.

The Iron Palm embodies both qualities of the hard and soft type.

In the year 1928, Mr. Ku Yu-cheong of Kwangsu Province sojourned to Kwantung to popularise the art of Chinese Boxing. It so happened that at that time in Canton, there was a Russian strong man who was giving an exhibition of his prowess. The Russian owned a magnificent horse and proudly made an offer of a rich reward to anyone, who could subdue the animal. Many experts in the Chinese Boxing Art made their attempts but, many of them were injured in the process. Mr. Ku, unable to tolerate any further humiliation of his colleagues, took up the challenge. In a matter of seconds, he succeeded in delivering a single slap on the animal's back whence, the animal out of sheer agony collapsed on the floor and after a few pitiful snorts, died. According to Master Lau Fat-Mang of the Eagle Hand School, who was present during the incident, a post mortem dissection was later performed on the horse. The findings of that post mortem showed that there was no external sign of injury but, the internal organs of the animal were Split and it's backbone revealed a large bruise. If what was described was true to the facts, then Mr. Ku was a master of the soft type of Kung for, it is not possible to inflict internal injury without external signs with the hard type.

There are in fact many different variations of that famous story. All involve a contest in which the horse was killed with a single slap and some describe that the horse delivered several deadly blows with its hooves before being struck and killed.

Age and Iron Palm Training

Age of the practitioner is not of consequence. If there is consistent training, success can be expected. Exceptions to this rule, however, do occur. In training in the soft type of Basic exercises, a younger person is more suitable, especially one who is under the age of twenty. This is because youth without the pressures of work and finances to attend to, is usually devoid of worries. He can thus concentrate and with full youthful energy to assist him success is the most likely outcome. An older person may need to be conditioned with meditative techniques to rid the body and mind of accumulated stress. However, an older person should prove more suitable to the hard type of basic exercises than a younger person. This is because the hard type imposes a great strain on the physique. On the other hand, an older person whose development is already complete is not likely to suffer adverse effects.

Training in the Basic Exercises (Kung) in relation to Medication.

External "Kung" training brings with it the potential to cause injury such as torn skin, cuts and bruising. This is a consequence of jabbing the hands directly into a container of Steel Shot. There is a so called indirect method which entails striking canvas bags filled with the same materials. Using the indirect method eliminates most of the potential for immediate injury. The indirect method I am going to recommend, is comparatively a more natural method but, even this method, if unassisted by Dit Da Jow medication, could lead to interference with the Qi circulation and cause pain, swelling and bruising. If carried too far, the stagnation of blood in the fist and fingers, can hamper the movements of the arms and can even cause injury to the internal organs. To prevent such injury, it is necessary, before the commencement of training, to wash the hands with the right type of medication. This medication must be given sufficient time to act in order to enable it to penetrate into the ligaments and flesh so as to give protection to these tissues and to increase their resistance to trauma. In this way, even if greater force is exerted, there would be no danger of bleeding or painful bruising.

Before during and after training massage the liniment into the flesh and use it liberally. Allow the liniment to soak into the skin then apply more and massage deeply. By use of liniment the progress of training can be accelerated and made safer. Bruises will heal much more quickly. "Kung" is inseparable from the use of medication.

The three important requisites in training.

In traditional Iron Palm training there are three requisites.

1. Gradual Progress

2. Perseverance
3. Sexual Temperance

Gradual training and progression is common in most physical development methods and in this respect Iron palm is no different. You must slowly condition your body to gradually withstand the vigour's of Martial Arts. A minor injury may cause a temporary obstacle to conditioning but a serious one may cause death or disability.

Injury is common in younger men who are overly enthusiastic and over exert themselves. Self discipline is the quality that must be drawn upon to prevent this. Iron Palm itself is a proven technique so any ill effects are usually the fault of an overly zealous student, one can not blame the method. Gradual progression and self discipline will protect you from much harm. An example is the student who from the outset strikes the bag with full force, thinking that in doing so he is preparing the hand for a full force strike against an opponent. In a short time this student will be able to break the bricks but not long after that will experience serious joint injury and possible broken bones. There are also concerns for damage to the "chi" energy flow and meridian stimulation. A student following gradual progression will take longer initially to perform breaks but will eventually be capable of far superior breaking without sustaining injury.

As self discipline and gradual progress are requisites to Iron Palm, so too must perseverance be practised to attain the goal. Even though a minimal amount of at least 30 minutes per day is required most people will eventually stop training at some point. 30 minutes to one hour per day, every day is the requirement and without this commitment Iron Palm can not be achieved. Iron Palm is a simple art to master if you apply perseverance. By giving up you become no better than one who has never trained at all. It is rare to see one's efforts unrewarded when there is perseverance.

Sexual temperance seems an unusual suggestion in this age of sexual excess and openness. But consider the energy and focus you are expending upon sex that could be channelled into actually useful activities. This is the traditional view. Modern science shows that sexual activity does have some advantages for physical and mental health so you must find an appropriate balance. Martial Arts aim at the conservation of strength, energy and vitality.

The different schools and their methods.

There is no single regimented system of Iron Palm but there are many various schools and implementations. Each practitioner will over time develop his or her own individual training regime. It is in this way that the various schools of Iron Palm originated. Generally all of the schools can be classed as direct and indirect methods.

We have discussed the direct method in which a large bucket containing mung beans is used to condition the hands by jabbing into the beans while standing in the horse stance. This is known as the "sinew changing" method. Once the hands are jabbed into the beans the hand is grasped and raised out holding a handful of beans. The hand is then slapped on the surface of the beans and the process repeated. The student will wash the hands in liniment at the end of the training. Other methods involve dipping the hands into very hot water prior to the jabbing. Another method involves slapping a block of timber daily for a long time until a groove is worn in the wood, then a stone is slapped directly every day for many years. With the Direct method the trainee's hand is likely to take on a rough and coarse appearance

Training with the indirect method is quite different from the above. Instead of a container, a canvas bag is used. The inside of this bag should contain mung beans. During training, the bag is hung up by a rope. The trainee should then step forwards and slap the bag with his open palm. Next, he should then slap it with the back of his hand. Both these movements should be regarded as it single movement. After a training session, the hands are again immersed in medication. Training should be done thrice a day, in the morning, afternoon and evening respectively. After a year the beans should be more or less broken up. They are then changed for new beans and an equal quantity of steel shot, is added. After another year of training, most of the peas would again be broken up and, this time only steel shot is employed. Training is then continued for yet another year.

If further training is required all that is necessary, is to continue training with steel shot alone. The indirect method of training, does not give rise to coarse and ugly hands and unless the hands are subjected to closer scrutiny, it is difficult to make out their difference from those of a normal person. The Indirect method is therefore the better method.

The 97 Day Method.

It is not advisable to employ too rough methods in training the palm. The method to be recommended is a gentle one and is a derivative of the indirect method. Gentle training is preferred to protect the hands from arthritic damage. The following method trains the hollow of the palm and the back of the hand, but also the finger, the base of the palm and the outer side of the hand as well.

The force utilised includes Slapping, Throwing, Cutting, Stamping and Dotting etc. Besides, only 97 days are required for mastery and achievement of the art does not result in coarse and rough hands. The method of training is as follows:

Equipment:

A bag made of two layers of course cloth, measuring two feet long and one foot wide, filled with steel shot to a thickness of three inches. If no iron filings are available an equal quantity of mung beans should serve the same purpose.

The bag is then placed on a table or bench, which should be of such a height, that it reaches a level slightly below ones navel. (Level of the Dan Tien)

Method:

1. Slapping Method.

When slapping, it must be realised that the whole hand is utilised. (This includes the palm and the fingers.) Raise the hand to a height, which is at the same level as the crown of the head. Then focus attention on the hollow of the palm and slap downwards on the bag.
Note: When training make sure that the shoulder and the whole arm is relaxed. Avoid exerting strength.

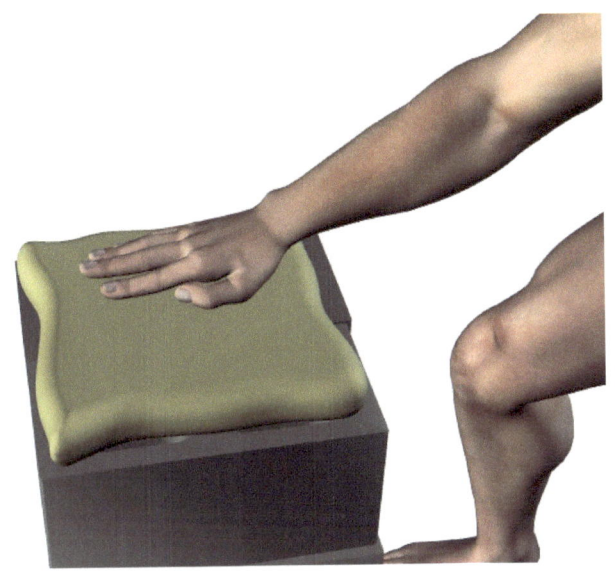

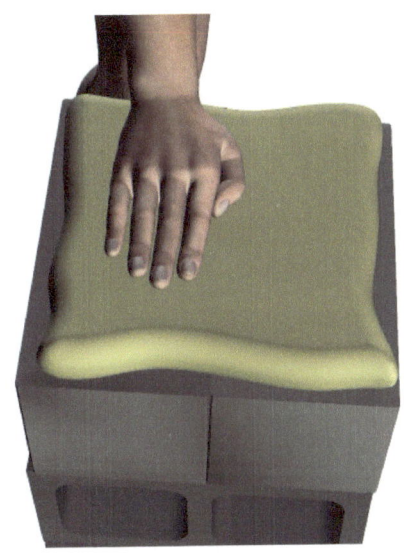

2. The Throwing Method. In this method, the back of the hand is utilised for the purpose.

   After performing the 'slapping' method, raise the arm up. Then focussing one's mind on the back of the hand, 'throw' it on the bag, as shown.

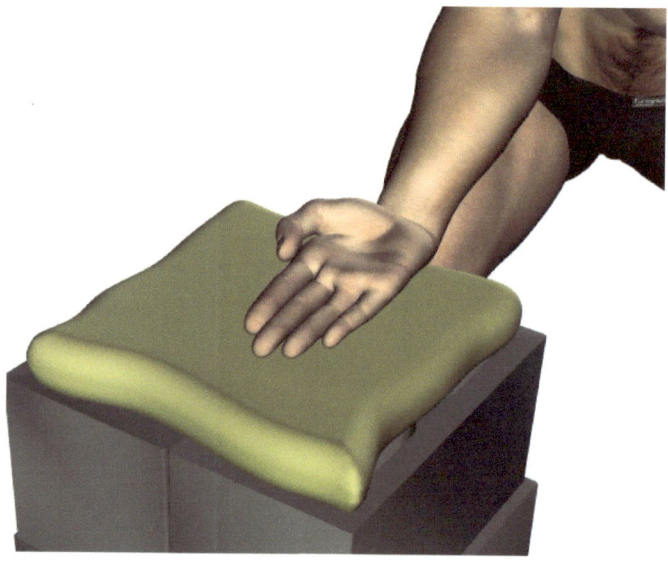

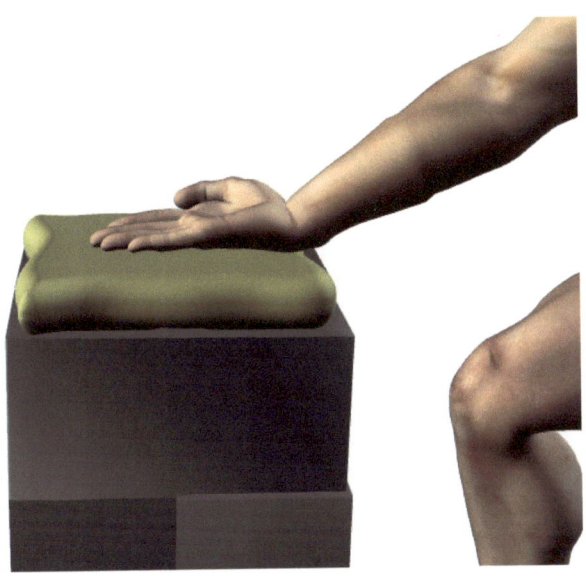

3. The cutting method. In this method, the side of the palm is made use of.
   Raise the arm upwards. Then, focussing attention on the side of the palm, 'cut' downwards on the bag. This cutting movement is similar to chopping on an object with a knife.

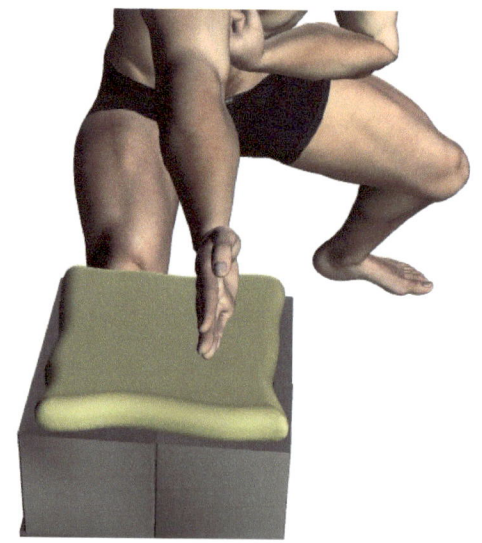

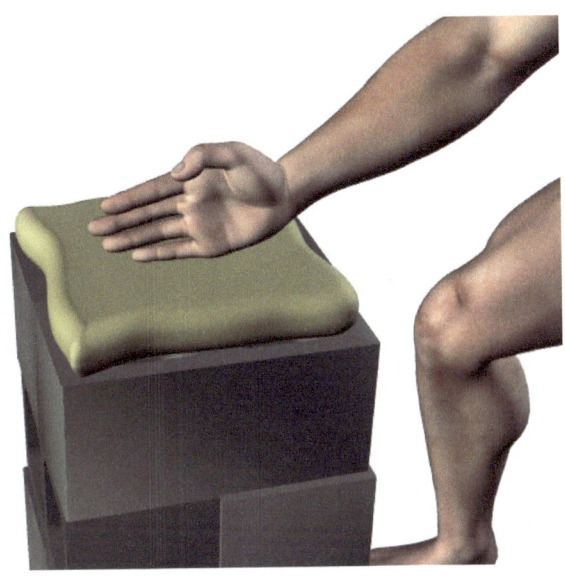

4. The Stamping method. The base of the palm is employed for this method. First raise the arm up. Then, concentrating on the base of the palm, 'stamp' it downwards on the bag.

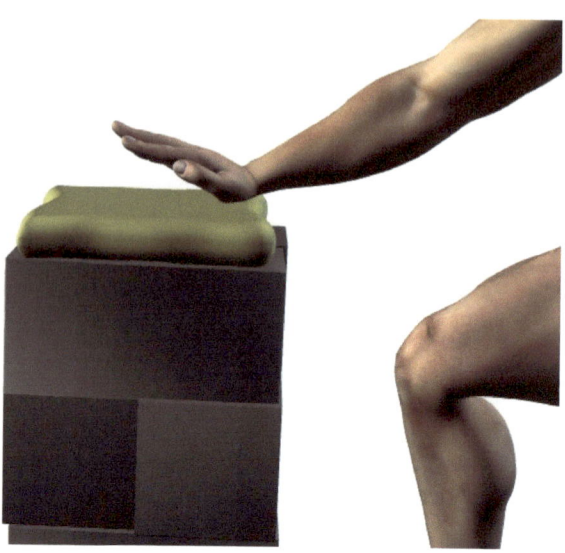

5. The Dotting method. The tips of the fingers are made use of in this method. Raise the arm then flex the fingers of the hand, focus attention on the fingertips, relax the arm and shoulders and `dot' them downwards.

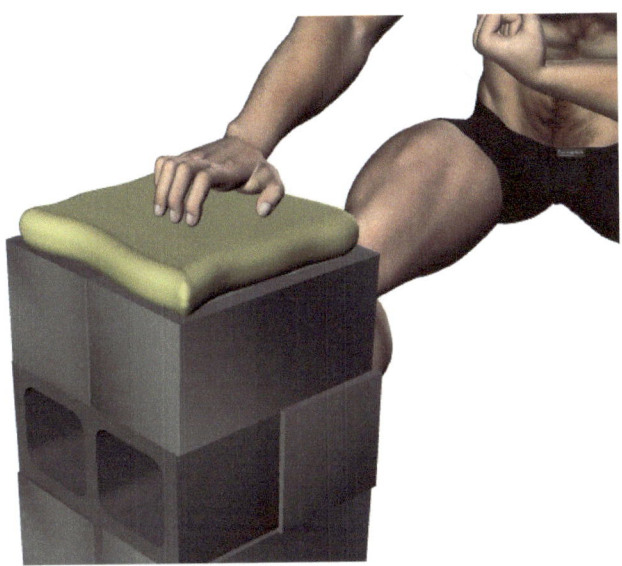

The above five methods should be regarded as a single exercise. At the beginning, one should measure up to one's ability and train only thrice a day namely in the morning, afternoon and evening. Do not exceed three periods in training and at each period, one should not do more than five exercises. After each exercise, medication should be applied before proceeding to the next.

Medication:

Dit Da Jow (Fall Hit Wine) is the special Chinese liniment made especially to compliment Iron Palm. Dit Da Jow is as old as the Iron palm itself. It is to be massaged liberally into the hands and lower arms before, during and after training as required. You must not train without massaging the Jow. Much information on Jow and massage follows later in this book.

Precautions:

1. Be careful of dust from your training bags. You certainly do not want iron dust in your lungs as Iron is a deadly toxin that can only be removed via venesection. A double thickness Iron Palm bag can go a long way to prevent this as can lining the inside of the bag with duct tape. Breathe through the nose or train outdoors.

2. Avoid striking with the muscular strength of the arms and shoulders. You are simply dropping the hand and slapping the bag with far less than maximal exertion. Force can be exerted by the wrist and palm in a whip like manner. This is a prudent skill to master as it will enable you to perform superior breaks at a short distance. This is the true skill of advanced Iron Palm and one that users of brute force will never attain. You will also protect the bodies internal energies training in this way.

3. Concentrate when you are training. Use it as a meditative practise.

Other measures:

After a session, rub both palms against the knees until they are warm. Get up slowly from the straddle horse stance, relax mentally and then walk about for a certain length of time. Simultaneously, lightly swing both palms about and also gently kick the legs forwards a couple of times, to relax the tension on the ligaments, and to normalise the circulation to the limbs.

Testing out:

The first 97 days or so are an introductory period. You should anticipate training for many years if not forever. However if you have trained diligently 3x per day for 30 minutes per session you may at this time begin to practise breaking. If you wish you may wait until a later time to do the breaking, months or even years. Its your choice. In the past testing was done on bricks, but the Chinese bricks were softer than our modern ones. Its better to use rectangular concrete capping blocks 1.5 - 2 inches thick. Make sure the blocks are dried through as hydrophilic bonds made by water make them harder to break.

Do not expect that you can simply break block after block immediately at this stage. Some may be able to do this and more so if they employ brute force. But we are training Iron Palm not brute force. So expect to strike the block many times without a break. Eventually the breaks will come. Be patient and persistent. After some weeks you will be able to break nearly every time. At this point you may add a second block. Do not perceive a strike that does not break as failure. Perceive it as a training strike as you develop your power and technique on the blocks. Perseverance is the measure of success, not a pile of broken rubble.

First, use the 'Stamping' method and in coordination, with the body, stamp the palm on to the middle part of the blocks. This way, the blocks would give way. Following this, employ the cutting method. Then consecutively use the slapping and throwing methods. If one could break the blocks by all the mentioned methods, the next step is to use two blocks. Later wooden boards should be used. When both blocks and boards can be broken, one's hands are then ready for use.

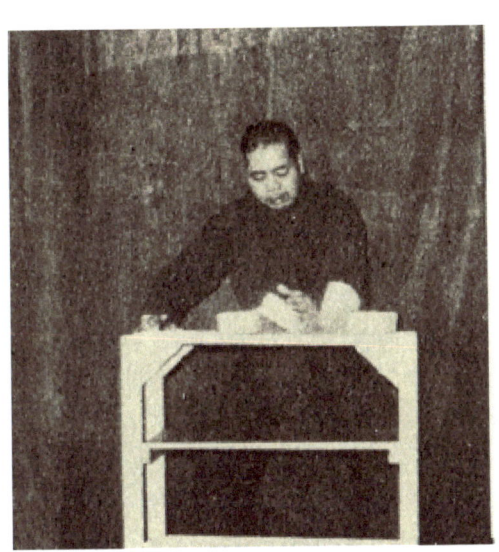
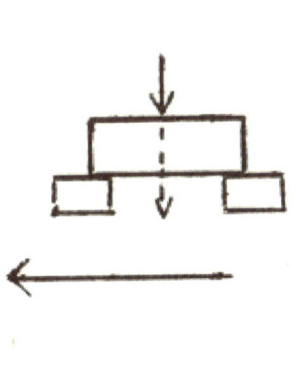
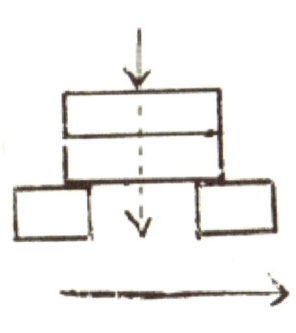
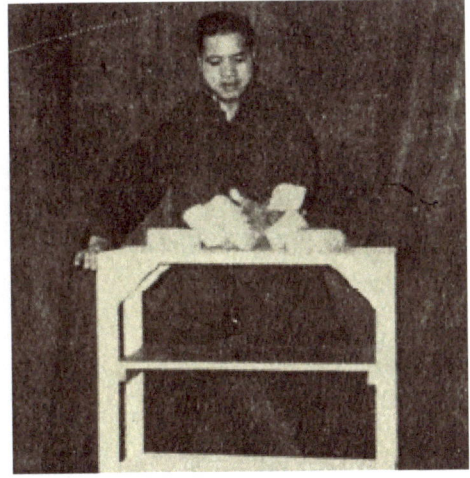

The final method shown should only be tried when the other methods are successful, Note: When stamping with the right palm downwards the left palm which supports the brick must be lifted upwards in co-ordination.

This breaking phase will also take many weeks to master, At first perhaps 90% of your attempts will fail but after 3 months of diligent and careful breaking practise you should be able to break 90% of the time.

Internal training methods.

If you continue to condition using the external methods your power will continue to increase. There are people that can break a solid 6 inch block of concrete. So certainly as you continue your power will develop but at some point you will meet the limit of your physiology.

Also at certain times you will need to miss a training day either through injury or other commitments. The time will come when you are ready to learn "Internal Methods" that draw upon internal energies. Electromagnetic and kinetic energy are what we usually mean when speaking of "Chi", "Qi" or "Ki". The human body has a genetically determined electro physiology system that was not discovered by western science. Western science has proven its existence however in scientific terms. So the meridians and points of Qi Gong and acupuncture are a physical reality and are not symbolic. The meridians are not abstractions of the nervous system but are real electromagnetic channels that are the same in all people just as are the skeletal system and the circulatory system, hence it is part of our genetic code.

The ancient Chinese and Indians also determined many of the functions of this energy system and how to utilize it. We in this case want to use it for Iron Palm training. The exercises suggested here are a brief introduction to internal Iron Palm as the theme of this book is external training.

It is possible to break using internal methods alone but this takes longer to learn.

The salient features in training:

1. During each movement, make sure that breathing is coordinated. At the same time, a conscious effort is exerted to focus attention on the palm.

2. Breathing must be natural. It must be deep, silent, soft and long and must above all be not too rapid nor too slow in tempo.

3. Irrespective whether the movement is a lifting or a pressing one, the tips of the elbows must face outwards (in relation to the body) and the fingers must be held close together.

4. During a lifting or a pressing movement, the knees must be straightened, for only thus would blood circulate from the Tan Tien to the two sides of the chest and then to the two palms.

5. In pressing or lifting, mentally focus attention on the palms. While lifting, imagine that one is holding up to the sky as if, "it may fall" and while pressing, imagine that one is pressing on a mountain, which is about to "upturn".

6. During training, there must be concentration. A conscious effort must be exerted and breathing must be quiet.

7. After a training session, post training exercises must be done as when one is training for the Iron Palm.

8. This "Internal QiGong" method has a limited number of movements but, it would suffice, if one could practice it twice a day.

The "All Round" method itself.

1. When training, stand at attention. The lower limbs must lie held close together. Stare horizontally and straight ahead. The left palm is made to face upwards, while the fingers of the Left hand are pointed to the right. Then, in coordination with inhalation, the left hand is lifted upwards, as if it were lifting the sky. The right palm is held downwards and the fingers of this hand are pointed to the right. The right hand is then pressed downwards, as if it were pressing on the ground. When the movements are at an end, exhale and relax the whole body. This is regarded as the first stance.
Without changing stance, perform the movements of lifting and pressing thrice.

2. Following the above, do the same movements but in the reverse, the right hand is used for lifting and the left arm for pressing. This is regarded as the second stance. Also perform these movements thrice.

3. Following the above stance, lower the right arm downwards, so that now both arms lie on each side of the body. Then, in coordination with inhalation, lift both arms upwards as if they were lifting up the sky. When the lifting n movement is at and end exhale and relax the whole body. This is regarded as the third stance. Perform these movements thrice.

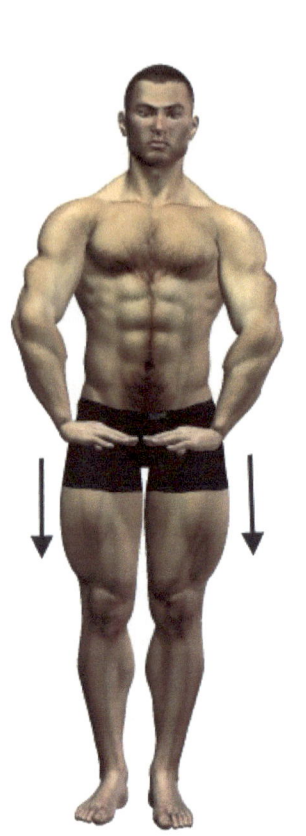 

Note: The all around method is very similar to Chi Kung exercises "Lifting the sky" and " Plucking Stars". In addition to these "Pushing Mountains" can also be performed.

To famiarize yourself best with these exercises I suggest you refer to youtube as it is not possible to show the correct form with illustrations alone. I have included some pictures to give you a basic idea of the postures but video will show the correct movements.

These methods alone do not represent a complete system of internal training. They will however assist in your development and control of internal energy.

Pushing Mountains

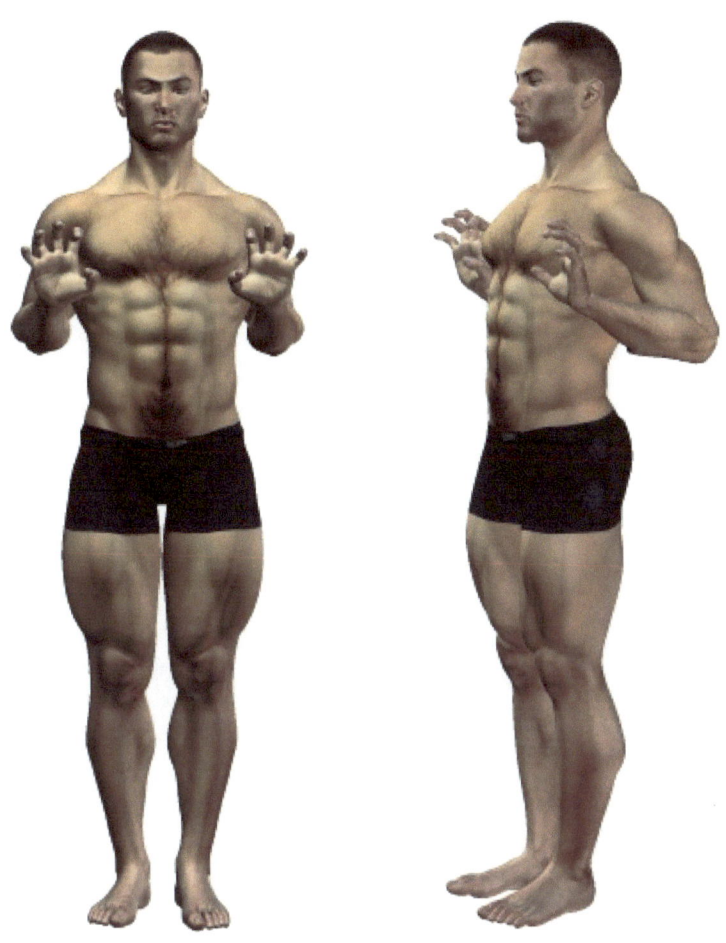

Plucking Stars

Lifting The Sky

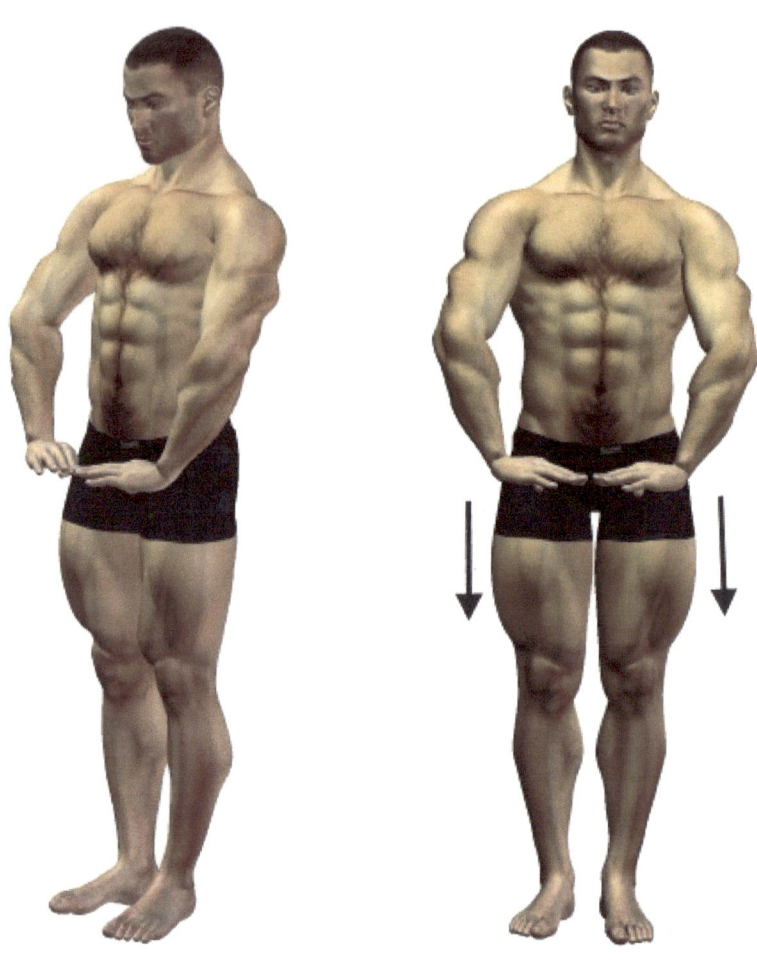

The Chi must emanate from the Tan Tien.

The Dan Tien is a point 3 inches below the navel, which is at the body's centre of gravity. For physical practise it is the most important energy storage centre in the body. If Chi can he mustered in this region, one's footwork will be stabilised, relaxation can be more easily induced and Chi can be better coordinated. These, it must be emphasized, are the basic requirements of the Inner School.

"Strength must permeate to the hollow of the palm."

Ones energy must be drawn to the palm when striking. This can be done in two ways. By directing the Chi or by employing force. As our method is external we employ force to direct the energy into the palm.

Methods of Ancient Chinese Gong

There are some documents remaining from years of communist oppression regarding ancient Qi Gong and original martial arts. Many were destroyed.

Many of the 72 methods are strength exercises inferior to versions developed in modern western weight training and bodybuilding. We will cover those here also. My advice is to complement your martial arts with bodybuilding, power lifting and a jump rope or kettlebell cardio vascular program.

We will now examine some methods of Gong briefly so that it you wish you may use these in your personal program.

Bamboo Leaf Hand

This is the very method we use in Yuan Chu Cai's training with the hanging bag. Fitting to mention it first.

The filling for the bag is the same as with all other bags in this book. First fill with mung beans for 3 months, then small round stones for 3 months, then with steel shot for 3 months and finally with steel ball bearings. With this method more weight is added every 3 months once you are on ball bearings. Add another 10 kg each time. Start with 15 kg - eventually you will be striking over 200 lbs. Use the exercises covered later in this book and you may do boxing and Muay Thai style strikes on the bag also. You will definitely require Chinese liniment to reduce bruising and damage – remember it is not required to strike with full force on such a hard target for the conditioning to be effective. Very few if any Muay Thai fighters will match your power if you train in this way.

As you can see from the illustration one aspect of this training is a palm strike that pushes the bag. Thus greater weight will develop greater power.

Palm, fist, chop, shoulder, hip, head, shin, knee, thigh, foot, forearm and elbows can all be trained on this bag. Primarily this exercise is for the palm and will take 4-8 years to truly master.

Two Bag Practise:

> Push the first bag off then turn and strike the other bag. Alternate from bag to bag as they swing in unison. The bag ropes can be connected near the top to assist with this. Blows with all body parts can be used.

Sand Bag Training

Yuan Chu Cai has us join two bags to swing together but this method goes beyond that. Ten bags are used to expedite co-ordination and fighting skills against multiple opponents.

Multiple body parts can be used and as one bag swings from a strike another can be struck and so fourth.

The bags them selves are arranged into a ring around the martial artist just as in the drawings. Assuming the bow & arrow stance a bag is struck and struck again when it swings back. Once this method is mastered two fists are used to strike two bags at once.

Then each hand immediately strikes a returning bag. As you can imagine this will develop great co-ordination. High speed and continuity are to be aimed for. The next level is to strike out in multiple directions still with two hands. Opposing bags in succession. Right, left, front and back.

As we discussed for the single bag, once hand strikes are mastered other body parts can be introduced. Finally movement is introduced such as running and jumping while executing the strikes.

Iron Arm

Iron Arm deals mostly with the forearm but also the upper arm. There are several exercises that come under the category of Iron Arm training.

Training the forearm is a simple process of striking and massage combined with medicinal liniments.

Both the inner and outer fore arm are struck as well as the side edge.

The process is followed daily for a minimum of 30 minutes.

Sand Tube forearm rolling is covered in Yuan Chu Cai's book. A tube of bamboo is filled with sand or stones and rolled on the forearms. Later hardwood or a heavy steel bar can be used.

There is a similar exercise, which may be more painful initially. This exercise uses gravity and pressure rather that striking blows to stress the fore arms.

You must balance your body weight upon a bar using the forearms as in the illustration. The arms can be moved and rotated so different points are pressed. The body is raised and lowered rather than a single isometric contraction. Isometric contraction can be used if desired later. Sets and reps should be gradually increased.

You may progress from a flexible bar, to a stiff wooden bar, finally to a steel bar. As a final note on Iron Arm I have found that I can easily beat my forearms on the flat bag and often do this after my Iron Palm sessions. There are several hanging bag exercises for Iron Arm in this book also.

Iron Hand

In this section we can examine some methods for Iron Palm, Iron Fist, Iron Finger etc.

So you will learn of a few extra exercises that can be used.

Above are three different methods of training Iron Hand. In the first he is beating bare steel shot and then massaging in Dit Da Jow. The second shows the familiar Iron Palm method.

The third shows a method of beating a wood block for many months then progressing to stone, then steel shot.

Tornado Palm

Tornado palm entails using a large container initially filled with sand or rice. The hand is forced into the material and stirred around in a circular manner. As you can imagine this is hard work. Material is changed to beans, stones, steel shot then ball bearings over the months.

Finally one returns to sand and can move the sand without touching it. Be this by static electricity, air pressure or a similar force I am unsure.

Finger Gong Methods (One Finger Zen)

We employ these finger-hardening methods in our Iron Palm training on the hanging bag and we use the jabbing technique with a bucket of steel shot. Such exercise as illustrated above is trained every day striking at hard objects throughout each day. Eventually after several years the finger jab will become hard enough to use as a serious weapon such as for Dim Mak.

So far the methods of Gong discussed have been Iron Gong, now we will look at some of the ancient strength methods applicable to our Iron Qi Gong that have analogies with modern weight training and body building.

Ancient Chinese Bodybuilding and Strength Gong

Weight Vest Training

First a general form of weight training called Flying Gong. This entails the use of weighted garments to be used while walking or running distances. The modern day equivalent is the "weight vest" which is a very popular method for enhancing callisthenics and plyometrics.

Modern weight vests are available at up to 150 lbs and you can also get weighted shorts, ankle and wrist weights. I'm sure it will be possible to get weighted leggings also.

You may think it cheaper to simply use a heavy backpack but weight vests are ergonomically designed to distribute weight naturally and minimize stress on the joints.

This is a good overall method to compliment Iron Body training.

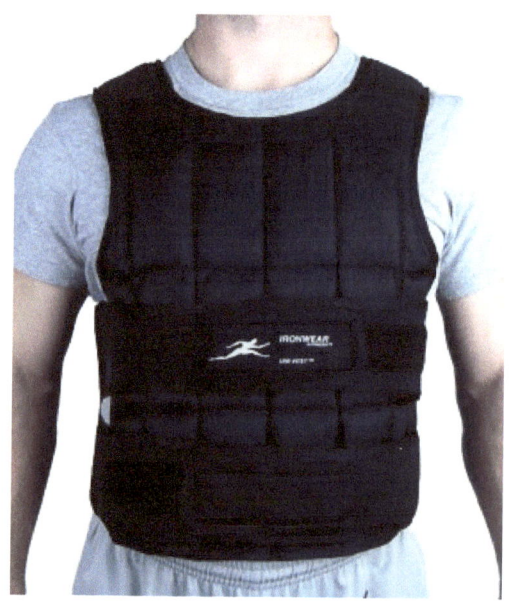

Wrist Roller

It seems funny that such a familiar bodybuilding exercise such as the wrist roller has actually been practised for hundreds of years. The Chinese used a jar and applied progressive resistance by adding weight just as weightlifters do today.

Sluice Gate

Here is another exercise this time for developing the deltoid muscles of the shoulders.

Easily emulated with a barbell or overhead press machine.

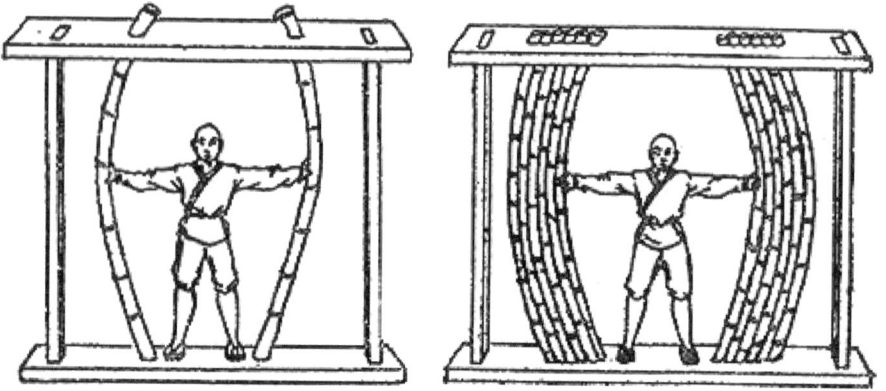

Another deltoid exercise using bamboo. Clearly the Deltoids, Trapezius and Lats are most put to work and I can't think of any modern equipment that can replace this apparatus.

Kettle Bell Training

The ancient Chinese liked to use stone weights and heavy padlock weights in largely the same way that modern kettle bells are used.

Hand Strengthening

Several hand-strengthening methods have been recorded.

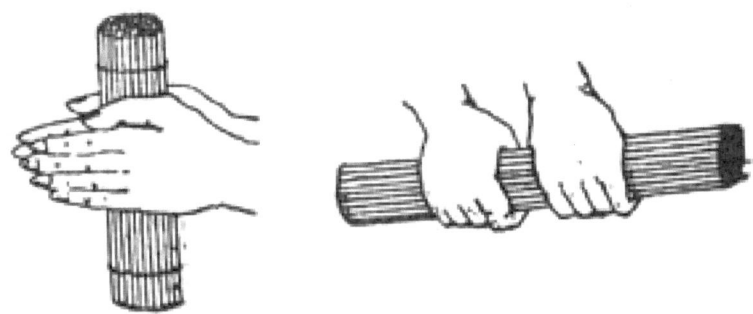

Rolling a chopstick bundle will strengthen the hand muscles over time. The hands rotate in opposing directions. Once strength is attained on wooden chopsticks you can change to metal ones.

In this exercise attempting to pull a post vertically from the ground each day develops the grip. This is an isometric exercise. After many months the post will finally be pulled from the ground and the grip will be much stronger. Modern day grip trainers use block weights to do much the same thing.

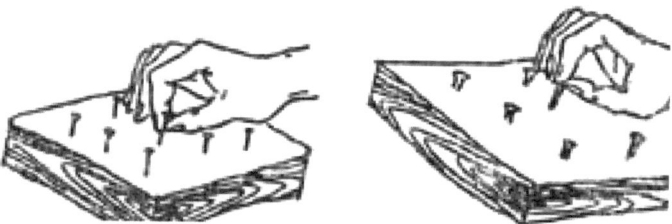

Pulling nails with the fingers develops finger and grip strength. Part three of this book covers grip and hand strength training in depth. This exercise will help with Martial Arts such as Chin Na.

There are many more Chinese exercises for developing both Iron Qi Gong and muscular strength and size. I hope that you understand then that modern weight lifting and bodybuilding are in fact part of traditional Kung Fu training. You should be lifting weights and developing your muscles and doing cardiovascular training in addition to the Gong Fu outlined in this Iron Palm manual.

Modern weight training and bodybuilding are a part of Kung Fu, not separate forms of exercise.

Cardiovascular conditioning can be done with the jump rope. This is because of the minimal amount of time required. Kettlebells are an even better choice.

Stretching is equally important and is a traditional part of Kung Fu conditioning. There are several high quality modern stretching programs such as "elastic steel", dragons door and Thomas Kurz. Look those up online as they are the three best programs. Once you have mastered those you can go on to add Yoga exercises.

www.stadion.com/stretching_scientifically.html
www.dragondoor.com/flexibility/
www.elasticsteel.com/

As a final thought upon modernization of Gong Fu consider the use of biofeedback electronics. This is equipment that can measure electrical and physiological systems in the body. Neurofeedback and infrared sensing of the brain can expedite rapid progress with meditation and visualization. Other forms of biofeedback can directly measure Chi in the meridians and points and also the polarities of energy in the body. Other forms can measure stress and muscle tension. Hypnosis can also be used to enhance progress as can traditional Chinese herbs and acupuncture.

Gong can be attained much more rapidly and to a superior level with modern technology and science. Perhaps this is a good topic for a different book.

Part three of this book will cover modern strength training methods for hands and forearm.

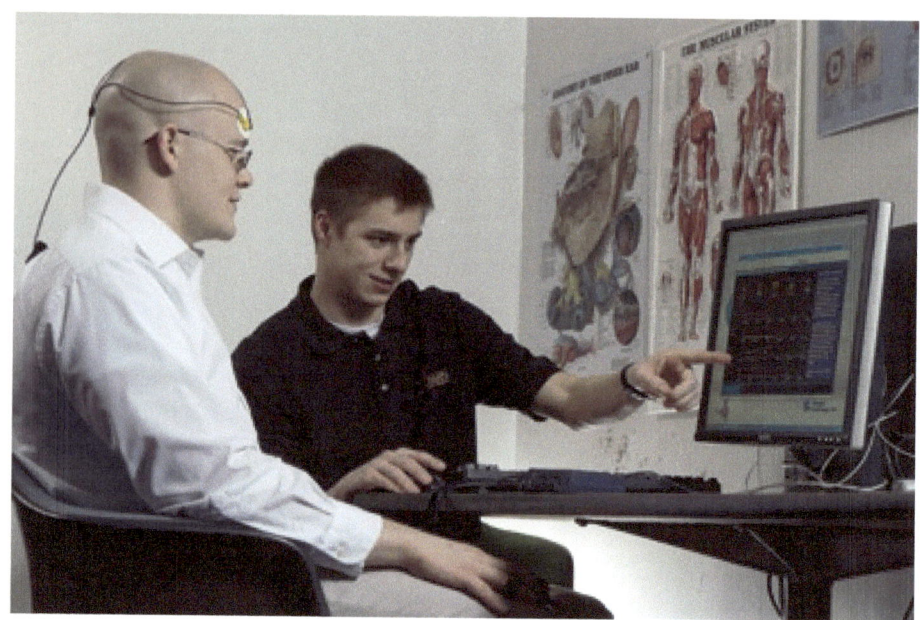

Section One: Iron Palm By Yuan Chu Cai

Yuan Chu Cai

MARTIAL Arts in China have traditionally been divided into hard and soft styles. This can be described as the tangible and the intangible.

The intangible is the inner style involving meditation and energy. The tangible outer style involves flesh and blood training. Both styles require many years of dedicated training.

There is a saying that "physical strength alone does not match the power of the fist". A smaller weaker person trained in Kung Fu may still defeat someone well developed and strong.

Why do the great attributes of strength and fitness not guarantee superiority in martial arts? It is a matter of dexterity, skill & conditioning. Physical superiority alone will not beat external martial skills. But in like terms it is argued that some one trained in fighting will not beat fully developed internal & external conditioning. This is because the later opponent has knowledge of CHI and the body's workings and will have conditioned his own body accordingly.

So we have basic physical fitness at the bottom, fighting skills as a middle ground and hard and soft Qigong as a higher practise.

But why is it so that a large, strong fighter with technical skills may have difficulty against an opponent with additional Qigong training?

The fighter who has mastery over CHI is like a giant in comparison. Such a fighter is rare. The practise of qigong is more difficult than technical fighting skills.

Those who practise qigong combat are far fewer in number. The training itself is less commonly known. Few people teach these methods of conditioning compared to the other methods. These skills are based upon effort rather than a natural advantage.

Every Martial Arts enthusiast should appreciate the importance of Qi.

Ways to develop martial qigong include Mei Hua Zhuang, Iron Palm, Qixingdeng, Iron Bell Shield / Iron Curtain, Iron Vest, Coin Dart (Jin Qian Biao) and Dan Wan Gong. None of these methods come quickly or easily but require time and dedication. First comes flexibility conditioning, then strength, muscle and bone. These are merely the foundation not the end of martial training.

To master these martial arts, you need to follow the right methods then put very much effort in the practice. You cannot accomplish the achievements without years of hard work. Practise fighting to make your body flexible and quick then practise Qi to make muscles and bones hard and tough - this is why people say:" Fist is the skin of Qi, Qi is the bones of fist, they rely on one another and support one another." Fighting skills & physical culture are thus complimented by qigong skills.

Martial arts are not easy. Real knowledge takes effort and time to acquire. Some new learners of martial arts are so conceited that they think they are masters after they have a basic knowing of several moves. Their conceit makes them nothing but jokes to a real master.

Previous books by Yuan Chu Cai include Shaolin Fist, Wu Dang Eight-Diagram Fist, Yue Fei Fist, Buddha Fist, Real Sun Sword, Mei Flower Sword, Liu He Rod. These books were based on his personal knowledge. It was from his articles in popular Chinese Martial Arts journals that this Iron Palm book was originally derived. This book is a collection of Yuan Chu Cai's skills and I think it will be very helpful to all martial art lovers.

Yin & Yang

Chapter 1

The Division of Inner Gong and Outer Gong.

It is often claimed that Tai Chi is an internal art while Shaolin Kung Fu is external. This is incorrect but does contain an element of truth. Zhang Sanfeng who was a student of Shaolin himself founded Tai Chi. Zhang left Shaolin and established Wu Dang Clan in South China, transforming Dragon, Snake, Crane, Tiger and Leopard, the five forms of Shaolin into Spirit, Tendon, Qi, Power and Bone as the Five-word Secret. Tai Chi was generated from Wu Chi (Nothingness, the origin of the universe in Taoism) and then generated Eight Diagrams. The moves of Tai Chi Fist look graceful, smooth and gentle, but this does not make it an internal martial art. Shaolin Kung Fu is fierce and tough but that does not make it an external martial art.

In ancient times, the Shaolin students isolated themselves from the outside world so their martial arts are called external while the Taoists tried to mingle with and preach people so Tai Chi is called internal martial art. This is why martial arts are divided into internal and external. Masters of internal martial arts (Qi) are not necessarily able to bear choppers and axes but could definitely resist common harm. This was called hard Gong.

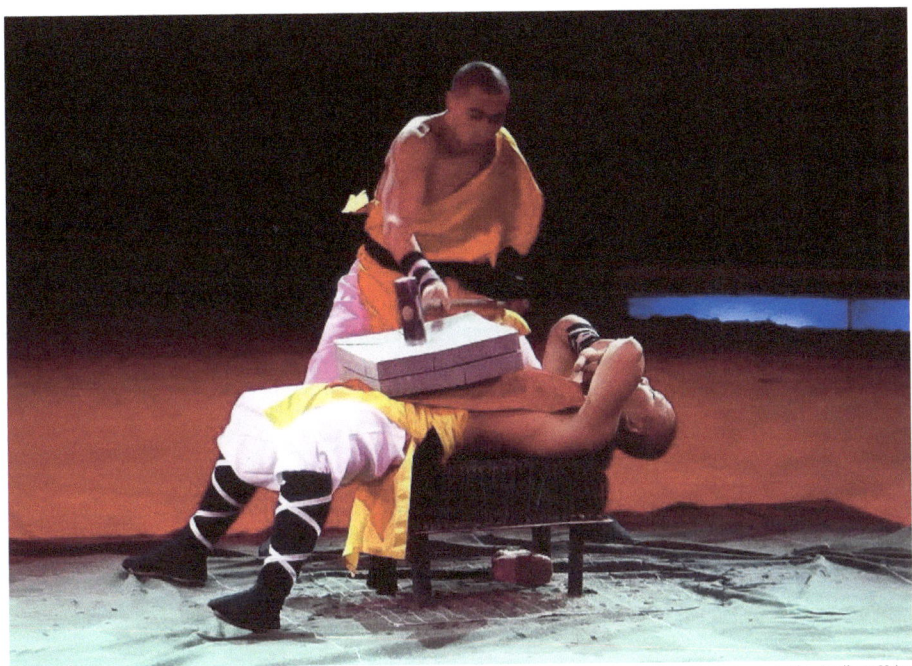

creative commons copyright, Attribute Usien

Shaolin Hard Gong Display

Section 1: Inner Qi Gong

1. Aestheticism: Sexual abstinence and seminal retention. Self-discipline in sexual behaviour is vital both in Qi Gong and regular martial arts conditioning. This gives one control over the emotions and lesser instinctive behaviours. It eliminates sexual distraction from training. Whether you are focusing on internal or external martial arts, you need to restrain desire and lust. Being puritan brings calm and calmness brings bravery (sensory & emotional control). When you engage in passionate activities you condition your mind to be vulnerable to primitive drives & emotions over which you have little control. Do not expose your desires, keep ascetic and stay away from distraction. Weeks of hard work may be ruined by sex overnight because sex damages Qi.

2. Concentration: To practise Qi, concentration is very necessary. Concentration brings deeper consciousness. Breath calmly and concentrate then you can distinguish the tiny changes and moves of

everything. To practise the ability of concentration, you could raise pigeons and watch them fly in the morning, reaching your sight as far as possible so later you could see & hear every move of the opponent as well as sense what happens behind you. Master Dharma lived in a cave in seclusion for 9 years, in the end he could sense the tiny sounds of ants as the mooing of cows. This is amplification of the senses is the effect of concentration.

The Immortal Soul of the Taoist Adept

3. Qi Control: Beginners are able to hold their breath in the Dan Tian (the lower part of abdomen) when standing still and inject the Qi into their limbs when moving. Qi Gong masters are able to circulate Qi

around their bodies, holding the Qi in the body when standing still and directing the Qi around the outside of body when moving. They do not inject the Qi into limbs but keep it in the chest and stomach, connecting the skull on the top and the arch of feet on the bottom. Qi is the most important element of the martial arts of Qi masters.

4. Building the Chi: Different martial artists have different types of Qi - weak, solid, gentle or fierce. Those of bad health must have weak Qi and those whose bodies are in good condition must have solid and sufficient Qi. Lack of Qi leads to weakness and excessive Qi may cause impulse and anxiety. Both of them are problems of Qi. All martial artists should learn handling Qi - enhancing Qi if it is weak and moderating Qi if it is excessive - this is why such martial artists always say "Keep the Qi of Heaven and Earth in the body."

   a. Enhancing Qi: People of weakness, without using any physical strength, keep the feet parallel, a little bit wider than shoulders and stand akimbo. Thumbs shall point backwards with the rest pointing forward. Thrust chest forward, head upright, eyes open, mouth closed and tongue pressing the upper jaw. Take in air through the nose and breathe out through the mouth slowly and repeatedly. Absorb the air in Dan Tian (the lower part of abdomen) then try to lift heels and stand on the tiptoes, repeat 30-50 times and increase the number day by day. This can make the Qi circulate better around your body.

   b. Moderating Qi, People of good vigour tends to have excessive Qi in the body. This causes anxiety, inflammation and unbalance. When doing martial arts, Qi wastes away even before moving. To avoid this, sit in meditation twice each in the morning and evening, legs crossed, arches of feet facing upward and palms facing up too at the level of the waist. Keep this position for half an hour to one hour. This benefits Qi moderation. This is called Luo Han (arhat) Qi Gong.

5. Adjusting the Chi: Adjustment of your breathing rhythm is good

for blood and Qi circulation and very helpful for Qi practice. Take a deep breath out through mouth for about 5 seconds; - breathe the air out from the chest for the first 1-2 seconds then the stomach for 3-4 seconds.

Then take in air with your nose for 5 seconds too. When practising martial arts, breathe out air when striking and take in air pulling fist back. In this way, the more you practise, the more Qi you will have in your body, the smoother the Qi circulation is.

Section 2: External Qi Gong

Once you have achieved internal martial arts (Qi), it is relatively easy for you to practise external martial arts (moves and fists) when practising with your fists; Qi will circulate in your body and be injected into your limbs - strengthening your bones and organs as well as muscles and tendons. Basic fistfight conditioning methods include lifting stone weights, conventional weight lifting, punching the sandbag, wooden dummy training and rolling with sand tubes. Lifting stone barbells and iron bars is relatively inflexible while punching sandbags and the wooden dummy is more effective, especially when practising 5 strikes and 6 Elbows. Nowadays people are mainly focusing solely on conventional weight lifting, this is a shame if it is all that is practised.

(1) Punching the sandbag (Bamboo Leaf Hand)

(a) A sandbag shall be made of canvas, approximately 50 cm high and the diameter is approximately 25 cm, stuffed with mung beans, sand or iron sand (small rounded stones, steel shot or ball bearings can also be used but start with mung beans first and after several months on each use harder material) In the first stage of practice the weight could be 12 kg, 18 kg for the second stage and 24 kg for the third stage etc. The rope on it shall not be too long - 60 cm is okay. The bag will be unstable and shake if the rope is too long. The bag should be at the level of the chest. Martial artists call this "Walking Horse Single Bag". After practising with this bag, make a bag of the same specifications and connect the two bags with a rope of 4-5 meters. Prepare two pulleys and attach one on each part 100 cm above the bag, with two bags 3 meters apart. The bags should both be at the level of stomach. Martial artists call this the "Connected Universal Bag".

Bamboo Leaf Hand is a hard force skill, which is used to increase the strength of the palms.

Technique: Hang a large canvas bag of iron sand as high as to your chest, then stand with one foot behind another. Use the palms to hit the sand bag. This method can improve the strength of arms and hands. At the beginning, the weight of the bag may be 15 kilograms, then be increased to over 70 kilogram with an increase of 10 kilogram.

(b) Practice Method of Walking Horse Single Bag: Push the bag with both hands, when it swings back, strike it with your head, then shoulder, thigh, elbow, knee, side punch and palm in turn. Three times a day and 30 minutes each time, the longer the better.

(c) Practice Method of Connected Universal Bag: Stand in between the two bags, push the one in front so the one behind swings toward you, then spin 180 degrees and push the bag that was behind, thus back and forth. This improves your co-ordination and reaction time and it betters your skills of fighting multiple opponents.

(2) Hitting the Wooden Dummy

(a) Use pine, camphor or other soft wood to create a human-like dummy model with a spinning axle on the bottom and a spring on the back so it could move back and forth as punched. Place padding on the head and chest of the model as protection when practising.

(b) Side-punch the model with right hand then left hand or kick with right leg then left leg.
Repeat these simple moves.

(3) Rolling sand tube

(a) Take a piece of bamboo of the diameter of around 20 cm and length of 60-80 cm, surface smooth. Put sand or iron sand inside. Make it 8 kg in the first stage, 12 kg in the second and 18 kg in the third. Increase the weight as strength grows. A thick iron bar or heavy hardwood can also be used at later stages.

(b) Keep your arms horizontal with the tube on them and lift and lower arms to let the tube roll along on them. Three times a week and 30 minutes each time. Then put the tube on the table, press your arms against it and roll it. You can also sit on a chair and put your feet on another chair, rolling the tube on legs. A long time rolling may make your wrists red and swollen, please use the following Chinese medicine. This medicine is necessary for all martial artists. Here is the recipe:

   Yunnan Sanqi: 25 metric grams

Yanhusuo: 20 grams
Mastic: 20 grams
Angelica sinensis: 25 grams
Ziyoutong: 20 grams
Myrrh: 20 grams
Teasel: 20 grams
Costus root: 15 grams
Sanguis draconis: 15 grams
Drynaria: 20 grams
Pyrolusite: 25 grams
Jiapi: 20 grams

Boil the herbs above with two bowls of clean water, when the water is boiling, add 500 g of leek roots and 500 g of white vinegar. Put the mixture in a jar and keep it for three days, then extract the juice - which is the Chinese medicine we need. Remember there are many commercial Chinese medicines available also.

Chapter 2

Outer Qi Gong

THERE are different names for Hard Gong, Arhat, 100-day Fist, Mix Qi Fist, Barrel Lifting Fist and so on, Though they have different names the methods are generally the same EG: rub and beat the body. This makes Qi and blood harmonious, muscles and bones solid. Pills and herbal baths can better the results. Applying the right method could help build your muscle sinew's strength and flexibility - making it resistant to knives and spears, even a car running over the abdomen. In this chapter we will learn all the methods.

Section 1 Massage/Beating

(a) Massage and beating

(1) Stand straight with your feet of the same width as your shoulders. Take in air (CHI) and inject it into Dan Tian, tongue pressing upper palate. Put the left hand on the waist. Rub the right palm on from 8th rib towards the nipple, then rub it back to the 12th rib then toward the nipple again. Do the same with the left palm. Repeat the moves above three times a day and 30 minutes each time. Practise for 49 days and this is the first stage.

(b) Beating

(2) After massage practice, you can practice beating. Make a canvas bag of the diameter of 8 cm and length of 45 cm, filled with mung beans. Use this bag on top of the head - knock it left right front back, half an hour every time. Hit the head with the bag gently from all directions.

Do the same to shoulders and shins. Three times a day and 30 minutes to 1 hour each time. This clears the chi channels in your body so Qi can better circulate. You will thus become able to direct the Chi throughout the body.

(3) After using the mung bean bag, try a bag of the same size, stuffed with sand or iron sand, steel shot and eventually steel ball bearings. Hit the body with the bag in the same way as you used the mung bean bag. After practice of beating with the sandbag, take a stick that is 8 cm long. Hit the body gently in the beginning then harder and harder (over a period of many months) This strengthens the body and after 365 days of practice the body can even resist penetration from knives and axes.

Section 2: Method of Medicine Manufacture

1. Method of Making Pills

(1) Pills:
Ginseng 25 g, white atractylodes rhizome 40 metric grams
Astragalus mongholicus 40 g, liquorice 20 g
Rehmannia glutinosa Libosch 50g, Angelica sinensis 40 g
Ligusticum wallichii 25g, radices paeoniae alba 20 g
Poria cocos 40g, Fructus Tribuli 25 g
Tu-chung 40g, teasel root 40 g
Fry the herbs with wine and pulverize them. Mix the powder with honey then make small pills with cinnabar cover. Store them in bottles.

(2) Instruction:
Every day take 12 to 24 pills with hot water 15 minutes before practice.

2. Method of Making Liniment

(3) Liniment:
Mastic 5 qian
Myrrh: 25 g
Sangzhi: 5 qian

Niuqi: 25 g
Centella asiatica: 25 g
Asiatic wormwood: 15 g
Fulongdan: 50 g
Costus root: 15 g
Yunnan Sanqi: 15 g
Wu Chia Pee: 25 g
Sanguis draconis: 25 g

Boil the herbs above with three bowls of water then mix with white vinegar and a bowl of leek root juice. Store the juice in a jar in case it loses effectiveness.

(4) Every day after practice, add a bowl of hot water into half a bowl of the juice. Wipe the mixture onto your body as liniment. It helps lessen pain and improves the effectiveness of your strike conditioning.

Chapter 3

Gymnastic Qi Gong

Q I Gong is the most important part of martial arts. Students of gymnastics start to learn the basics when they are young, which belong to Qi Gong too, like back flips. It helps you move fast when practising martial arts and fighting - Qing Gong masters could even
run partly up on a wall and walk on cliff faces. The Qing Gong exercises discussed in this section are what we consider to be gymnastics in the west.

Section 1: Walking on the Wall

(1) Knock two pegs of 15 cm in the wall, 40 cm away from each other and 1.6 meters above the ground. Stay 5 steps from the wall with no footwear. Take a right step first, four steps in total towards the wall then step the right foot on the wall and catch the left peg with the left hand, body straight - keep the posture for 10 seconds. Go back to where you were and repeat the practice. When you could hold the peg and keep the posture for 3-5 minutes, you have made it.

(2) Put two iron rods or bamboo pegs of 10 cm in the wall, the right one 2 meters above the ground and the left one 2.3 meters above the ground, 46 cm from each other. Step 5 steps back from the wall then run towards the wall with right foot stepped out first. Catch the right peg then step the right foot onto the wall, then reach the left hand to the left peg and hold it, body straight and feet press the wall. Keep the posture for 10 seconds. When you could hold the peg and keep the posture for 3-5 minutes, you have made it.

(3) Stay 7 steps from the wall and start with the left foot running towards the wall. Step the right foot on the wall when one step away from the wall and grip the wall with right hand, then step the left foot on the wall and grip the wall with left hand. Repeat this and you will finally achieve Gymnastic Qi Gong.

Section 2: Walking on the Tight Rope

(1) Prepare a thick rope that is just over 3.3 meters long, and 2 piles that are one meter long fixed into the ground, 3.3 meters apart, 75 cm above the ground. Tie string to the ends fastened. Make a "rope bridge". Keep your body straight and walk on the rope, arms reaching to sides to maintain balance. Keep your balance. If you can walk on it 100 times without falling off, you have made it.

(2) Prepare a thick rope that is about half size as the previous one, Make a "rope bridge" with the rope. Piles 16 ft apart, 3 ft above the ground. The practice method is the same as with the previous exercise. If successful then this Gong is done.

(3) Use iron wire to replace the rope to create a "bridge" and practise the same as the previous, same thing, distance 20 ft, 5 ft above the ground. Walk on the wire. Body straight, hands horizontal, like before. 100 times and walking like on the ground, the Gong developed is so excellent that it can't be imagined.

Section 3: Walking on Wooden Piles

(1) Use four 36 cm circumference wood trunks, 75 cm long, fixed into a square of four directions, 36 cm above the ground, 85 cm apart, when practising, left foot on the east pile, hands on waist/ akimbo, body straight, don't bend, two feet on the pile, better to use the front part of the sole, then right foot jumps to the south pile, left foot jumps to west, right foot jumps to north. Several times a day, early morning and night. Introductory Gong skills will thus take effect.

(2) Reduce the diameter of piles to 24 cm, increase the length to 110 cm,

75 cm above ground, 110 cm apart, use the same method. If possible practise using a weight vest, or similar body weights such as a heavy backpack, ankle & wrist weights etc.

Chapter 4

Iron Palm (Jabbing)

DURING human evolution and growth, before intellectual development, we attack and defend with our limbs out of instinct. This stimulates the brain development so that we humans later use our brains and limbs simultaneously. That is where martial arts came from - martial arts are skills of attack and defence with the limbs and other parts of body.

Ancient China was a place where martial arts prospered. To practise martial arts, the student must have a healthy and solid body so there are Iron Methods and Qi Gong that help strengthen the human body. But Iron palm has not been paid enough attention, this is not right - all martial arts are about limbs and every martial artist should strengthen the limbs before practice.

Before starting to learn Iron Palm, make sure you have the medicines mentioned earlier so the bruises, sprains and swollen parts can be cured.

Section 1: Fingers

1. Parallel Stance Downward Finger Stabbing

Vertical Insertion with parallel feet. Prepare a barrel of the length of 33 cm and the diameter of 20 cm, filled with mung beans in the first stage and 3 months later with iron sand. Place the barrel on a woodblock that is 33cm round and 45 cm tall. When practising, stand with your feet a little wider than shoulders, thumbs pressing palms and the rest of fingers kept together and stab your fingers into the beans or sand. Practise this move for hundreds of times each day, the more the better.

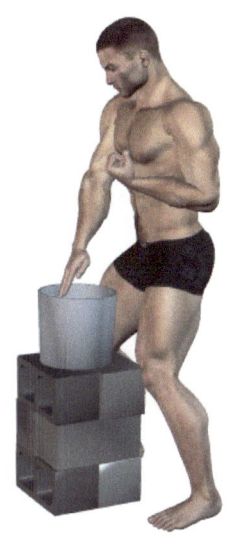

2. Left Hand Crouching Stance inclined Finger Stabbing

Place the sand barrel on a horizontal incline, put it on a 60 cm wooden bench, when practising, put the left leg in the front slightly bent and the right leg slightly horizontal bent down, have the feet at a right angle. Stab into the barrel, right hand protecting the chest, look at the sand barrel, direct chi all over the body, Jin/Chin/strength to the limbs.

3. Right

Hand Crouching Stance inclined Finger Stabbing

This is the same as the previous exercise using the opposite hand to stab the fingers into the mung beans. When practising this move, concentrate to circulate Qi around your body. Three times a day and at least 100 times of inserting each time.

4. Grabbing Method

(1) Grabbing with Angled Stance

Make a canvas bag filled with iron sand and place it on a woodblock of the length of 80 cm. Grab the bag then put it down with the illustrated stance. Use both hands in return, three times a day and 100 repetitions.

Iron Power Palm

(2) Parallel stance grab and lift method

Standing with parallel feet, grasp and lift the bag with the right hand and place the left hand on the waist. Hold Qi in the Dan Tian.

(3) Parallel stance grab and lift

Following the previous exercise, throw the bag out of your right hand and catch it with the left one. With all five fingers immediately grab it while placing the right hand on the waist, switch hands to throw and catch, first period 20 pounds. Practise 3 months add 10 pounds to make up 30 pounds, 3 months, then add 10 more for period 3 and practise 3 months, if your Gongfu is good the heavier the better, 3 times a day, 100 repetitions per time, you must persevere, this Kongfu, can practise finger strength, and add to arm strength, but strength and chi are the same.

Finger Thrusting

After the foundation of the former stabbing and grabbing, this is more powerful, after practising this it is no matter to strike brick walls and break them with a single strike. When fighting with others, you can win without a doubt.

(1) Double Thrust with Bow stance

Make a canvas bag about 36 cm by 20 cm, iron sand, steel shot or fine gravel inside, first 15 kilos for 3 months, then 20 kilos 3 months, then 30 kilos. The longer the better. If you feel finger strength increasing, you can increase the weight, tie a rope on the tip of the bag and hang it at chest height, when practising push the bag forward and when it comes back poke all 10 fingers into the bag, poke it away. Practise 3 times a day with 100 repetitions, switch leg positions, chi strength goes to limbs.

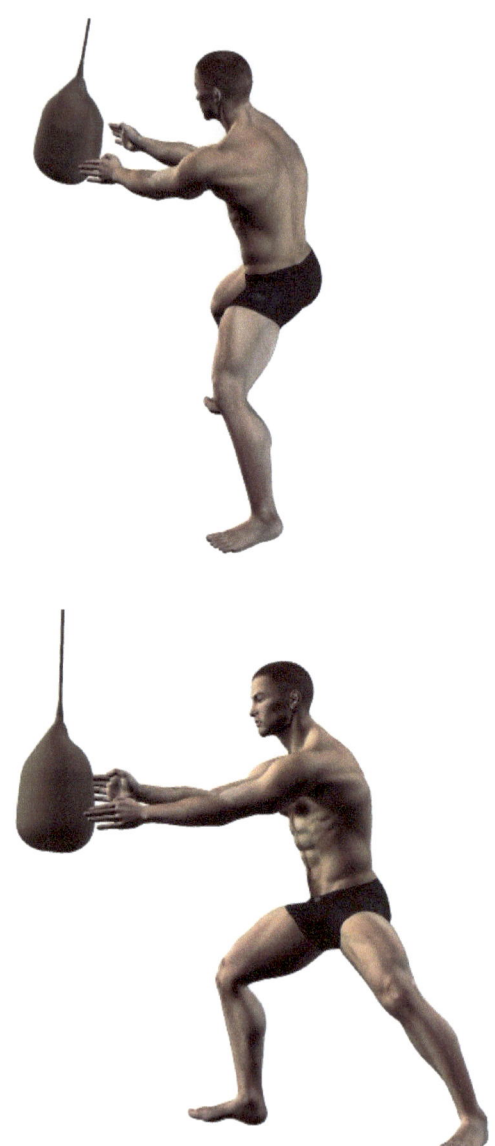

(2) Right Thrust with Hook-Step

Use the same bag and stand with a Hook-step. Thrust fingers of the right hand towards the bag then the left hand when the bag swings back. Three times a day and 100 hundred repetitions.

(3) Left Thrust with Side-Step

Stand with a Side step, body twisted towards the left at a small angle. Then thrust your left hand fingers towards the bag, and then use the right hand when the bag swings back. This builds two hands like steel and develops Kong fu for Iron Palm.

Chapter 5

Iron Palm (Slapping)

Section 2: Palm

THE practice of palm is the most important part of martial arts. As masters say: Palm is the mother of Fist and Fist only assists Palm. Usage of Fist comes from changes of Palm. Another saying from masters: 30 percent relies on Fist and 70% depends on Palm. Palm includes Hook, Lift, Block, Push, Raise, Chop, Grasp and Take.

(1) Parallel stance slap

Make a canvas bag filled with 10 kilos of iron sand or sand and place it on a wooden block that is 80 cm tall. Be in horse stance and twist the body towards the right by 45 degrees. Beat the bag with your palm. Use two palms in turn. Three times a day and 100 repetitions.

(2) Leftward Palm with Bow-Step

Stand with Bow-step and lift the left palm to the level of your shoulders. Beat the bag with the left palm horizontally. This is called "washing the tigers face".

(3) Rightward Palm with Hook-Step

Twist the body towards the right by 45 degrees. Lift the right palm to the level of your shoulders. Beat the bag with both hands in turn. Three times a day and at least one hundred repetitions. Inject Qi into the limbs.

3. Striking palm practise

(1) Horse stance Striking palm

Use the same bag as when practising Downward Palm with parallel feet. Enter the horse stance and beat the bag with the back of your hand, thumbs pressing against palms and the rest of fingers kept together. Use both hands in turn. When the skin is red and swollen, use the Chinese medicine created as instructed in previous chapters.

(2) Horse Stance Right Palm Back Hook

Raise the body a little from horse stance of the previous move. Put the right arm at the level of shoulders and beat the bag with the back of the hand. Keep Qi in the Dan Tian and inject into your limbs when beating.

(3) Left hand Reversed Palm with Hook-Step

Stand with a Hook-step and lift the right arm to the level of your shoulders. Beat the bag with the back of left hand. Use both hands in turn. After this stage the hands will be hard as stone and moves in the horse stance will be faster. This is the second step of Kongfu.

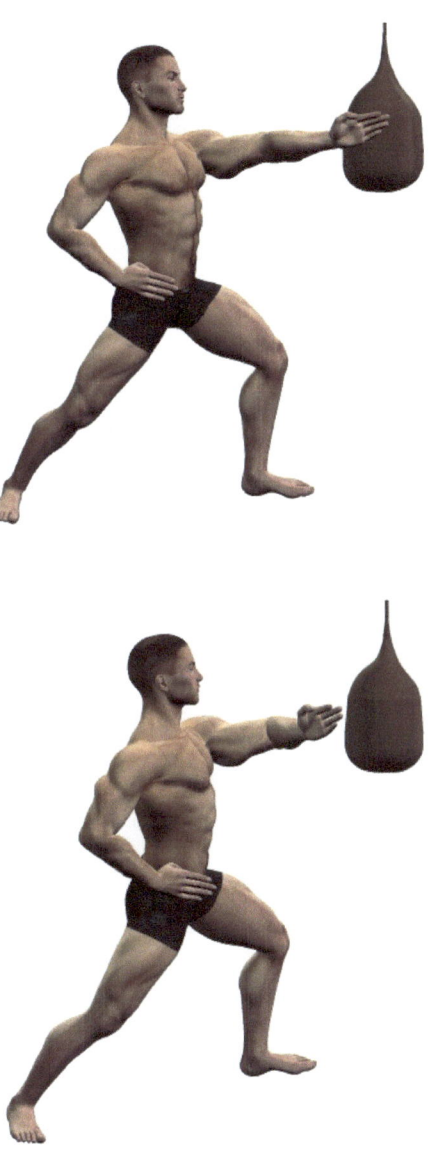

Right Hand reversed Palm

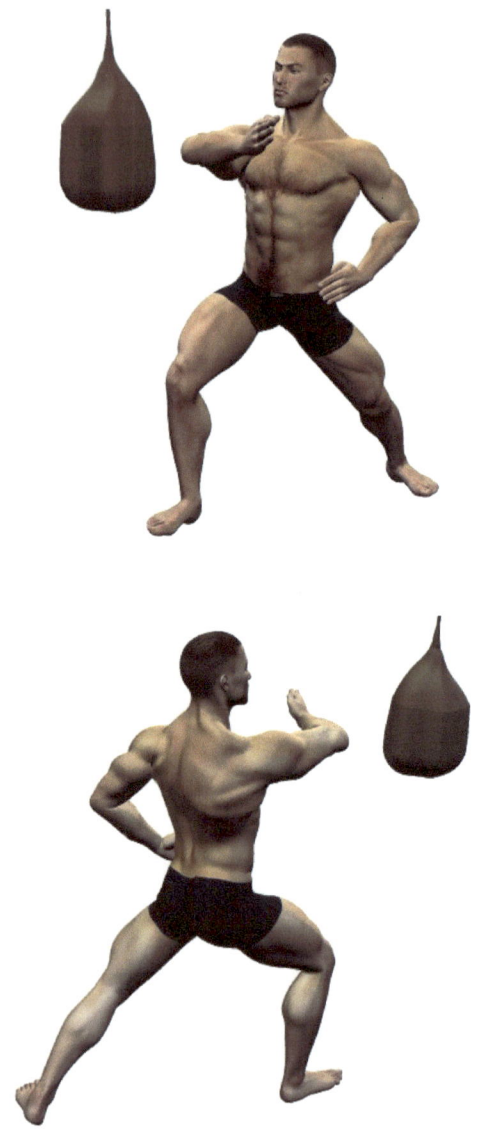

Knife Hand Bow Step

Section 3: Hand and Fist

Fist can be divided into long and short, Yin and Yang. Fist accounts for only 30% in martial arts, it is commonly used because it is relatively easy and practical for new learners. To master Fist, the upper, middle and lower parts of body must coordinate with each other, with the assistance of the horse stance.

1. Side Fist with parallel feet

(1) Thrust Fist with parallel feet

Use the same bag. Have parallel feet of the same width as the shoulders in the horse stance. Clench the right fist as hard as possible then punch the bag, with left fist pressing the waist. Eyes should follow the fist.

(2) Left Side-fist

From the previous move, then draw back the right fist and step the left foot forward. Lower the body and punch the bag with the left fist, right palm pointing upwards, like a phoenix bird spreading its wings.

(3) Right Side-fist

From the previous move, then draw back left fist and step right feet in front. Lower the body and punch the bag with right fist, left palm pointing upwards, like a bird spreading wings.

2. Thrust Fist with Hook-step

(1) Leftward Thrust Fist with Hook-step

Step out with the right foot, knee curved and make the left hand into a fist, with Hukou (a part of the hand between the thumb and the index finger) facing up. The left arm is at the level of shoulders. Punch the bag and eyes should follow the fist. Inject Qi into your fists and feet.

(2) Rightward Thrust Fist with Hook-step

From the previous move, draw the left fist back. The left foot steps in front and the right foot moves back. Keep the right arm at the level of your shoulders and punch the bag with eyes following the fist.

(3) Double Thrust Fists with Hook-step

From the previous move, when the right fist punches the bag away. Thrust both fists when it swings back. As time goes on, your two fists will become like a copper hammer or steel drill, they can then strike hard and break solid objects, this is the third step of Kongfu.

Practise the three moves above as a set.

Chapter 6

Elbow

Section 4: Elbow

THERE are 365 bones in the human body. There are 2 major bones in each forearm, which belong to hardest bones in the body. This makes the elbows as important as fists and palms.

There are many ways to practise elbows, like hitting with a bamboo stick or hitting solid concrete walls. But the most effective are the methods of sandbags and sand tubes. Here are more detailed explanations.

1. Sandbag Method

(1) Elbow Strike with Hook-step

Push away the bag with the left and use the right forearm to hit the bag when it swings back. The fist should be at the same level as the nose. Keep Qi in the Dan Tian and inject it into your limbs. Use both forearms in return. Three times a day.

(2) Leftward Push Elbow with Bow-step

From the previous move, when the bag is pushed away, use your left forearm to hit the bag, with fingers of the right hand supporting it and standing with Bow-step.

(3) Rightward Push Elbow with Bow-step

From the previous move, use right forearm to hit the bag, fingers of left hand supporting it and standing with Bow-step. This helps consolidate the muscles as well as enhancing defence capability so one can prevent any coming fist attack and can sustain any hand held weapon attack.

2. Arm Roller

(1) Rolling Arms with Bow-step

Make an arm roller of the length of 80 cm and the diameter of 40 cm, stuffed with sand or iron sand. In the beginning make it weigh 10 kilos, add 5 kilos after 1 or 2 months. Lift the arms and keep them straight. Roll the tubes on the arms back and forth. You can experiment with more weight and different materials, as you get stronger.

(2) Upper arm with parallel feet

Stand in horse stance. Lift the arms at the level of shoulders, Hukou facing up. Roll the tube back and forth. If the skin gets red and swollen, use Chinese medicines as instructed as before.

(3) Parallel stance roll lower side of arm

Place the sand tube on the woodblock and stand on lower horse-riding stance. Press the forearms on the tube and roll it. If the skin gets red and swollen, please apply the Chinese medicine as instructed in earlier chapters.

Iron Power Palm

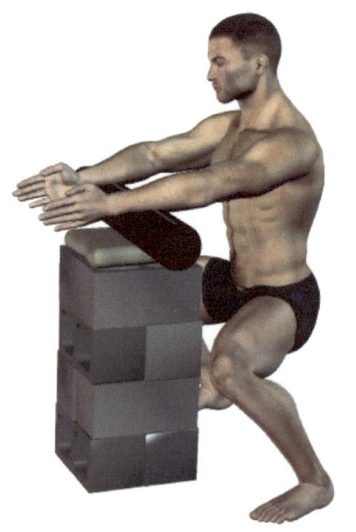

Five Feng and Six Elbows

Section 1: Method of the Five Feng

FIVE Feng (literally mountain top here meaning any sharp point or striking point), like head top, head back, shoulder joint, hip top, knee joint. Feng and Elbows are different but have the same effect. So they shall be practised simultaneously. They are especially effective when you are grappling and fighting close to the opponent or are locked or blocked by the opponent. So all martial artists should pay attention to them.

(1) Head Feng (use at your own discretion)

　　a.　Stance Practice. Take the bag as the target and hold it to make it stable with hands. Hit the bag with the head. Keep in down in the Dan Tian.

　　b.　Practical Usage. When the enemy is attacking in the face, you could use hands to defend and head to attack back. Pay attention to the leg, in case the opponent uses knees to attack.

(2) Head (back/side) feng

a. Stance Practice. Lower one side of the body to use the side of head to hit the bag. Use both sides of head during practising. Keep Qi circulating in the body and inject it into your limbs and head.

b. When being attacked or locked by opponents from behind, lower the body and hit the enemy with side/back Head Feng. If grabbed from behind, you can't move your arms, then press his hand, body down, right shoulder inclined, use your head to strike the chest, his grip will loosen, then you can use both hand and leg.

(3) Shoulder Feng

a. Stand in horse stance and lower one side of the body to use shoulder to hit the bag. Use both shoulders in turn.

b. When arms are being locked by the opponent, lower the body and use the shoulder to hit the opponent so arms are released.

(4) Hip Feng

a. Stand with Right foot in front and left foot behind, lower one side of the body. Hit the bottom of the bag with thighs.

b. When being hugged from behind, grab the arms of the opponent and hit with Thigh Feng. This is a common skill in wrestling and judo.

(5) Knee Feng

a. Stand on the left foot with right leg bent at the knee. Hold the bag with both hands and hit the bag with the right knee.

b. When your hands and that of the opponent's are grasping together. Pull the opponent close then hit him in the stomach with the Knee Peak.

Section 2: Method of the Six Elbows

(1) Sitting Elbow

a. Stand straight with fists above the waist. Hit the bag behind with your elbows.

b. When being locked from behind, use your elbows to hit the chest of the opponent so you can get free. This is the first method of escape.

(2) Side Elbow

a. Stand in horse stance. Keep your arms horizontal and fists close mid chest. Hit the bag with left elbow. Use both elbows in turn.

b. When being locked from the side, use the Side Elbow to fight back towards the chest. This would hurt the opponent seriously. This is the 2nd method of escape.

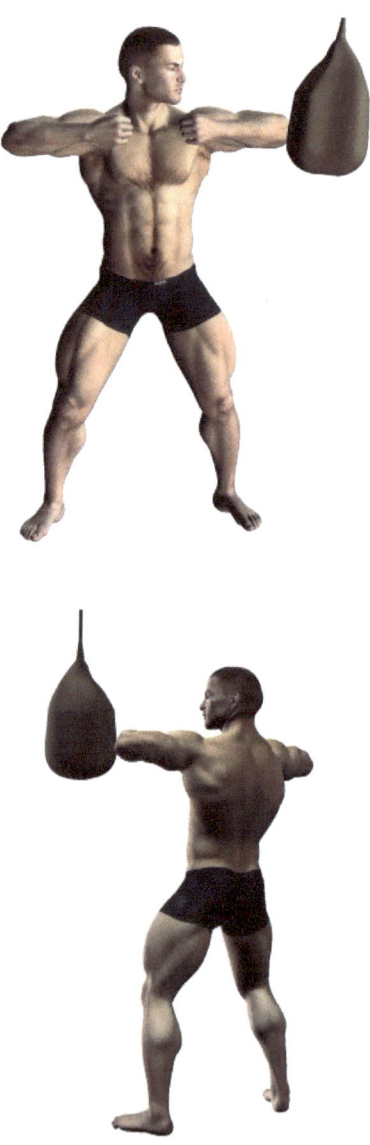

(3) Heart Elbow

a. Put the right foot in front and left at the back. Lower the body and hit the middle part of the sand bag with the elbow tip. Use both elbows in turn.

b. When the opponent is face-to-face with you, trying to catch and lock you, use Heart Elbow to hit the chest so the opponent backs off. This is the 3rd method of escape.

(4) Lifting Elbow

    a. Stand in horse stance and lower the body. Lift the right elbow to hit the bottom of the sandbag. Eyes follow the tip of the elbow.

b. When being blocked by the enemy from the front, lower the body and use Lifting Elbow to hit the opponent in the Qimen Accupoint.

This is the 4th method of escape.

(5) Pressing Elbow

Put your left foot in front and right foot at the back, clenching one fist in another. Hit the bag downward at the bottom. Eyes follow the elbow and inject Qi in limbs.

> b. When being locked from the front, take the right foot back and use Pressing Elbow to hit the Dujiao Accupoint of the opponent.

This is the 5th method of escape.

(6) Binding Elbow

a. Step the left foot in front and keep the right one back. Hit the middle of the bag with the tip of right elbow. Eyes follow the elbow. Keep Qi down in Dan Tian and inject it into the limbs.

b. When the arms are being locked by the opponent from the front, step the left foot in front, lower the body and hit the rib of the opponent with Binding Elbow.

This is the 6th method of escape.

Books on Martial Arts
Qing Ping Sword
Eight-Diagram Palm (Illustrated)
Iron Palm (Illustrated)
Judo
Extracts of Fists
Shaolin Fists
Karate
(Demonstrated by Master Yuan Chucai) Written by Yuan Chucai
Double Swords of E Mei written by Yuan Chu Cai
North Buddha Fist 1 book
Yue Fei Fist 1 book
Shao Lin Jianggang Fist
Mei Flower Sword 1 book
Chun Yang Sword 1 book
Liu He Rob 1 book
Chuanyun Umbrella of E Mei 1 book
Iron Palm (Secret Classic)
Quincuncial Piles (Secret Classic)
(Demonstrated by Master Li Yingang) Written by Li YInggang
72 Qinna 1 book
(Demonstrated by Master Liang Yongheng) Written by Liang Yongheng
Mixed Fist of Snake, Cat and Crane 1 book

Section Two: Iron Palm Secrets

THIS section of the book answers many common Iron Palm questions.

1. What is it?

- QiGong?

    Iron Palm is a form of QI Gong developed for the purpose of preparing the hands to strike with enhanced force without tissue damage to the practitioner. Closely related to Iron Palm are Iron Arm and Iron Shirt Qi Gong. The beating and massage methods used in Iron Palm are similar to those employed in Iron Shirt and medicinal herbs are applied to the hands also to ensure healing.

- Why Do It? - Is it necessary?

- To damage someone else more efficiently?

    Iron Palm will enable you to perform breaks that would not otherwise be possible and without damage to the hands. It is common for Iron Palm practitioners to be able to break multiple concrete slabs, coconuts and hence human bone. The skills developed in Iron Palm training are clearly potentially lethal and must be given the appropriate respect.

- Able to receive less damage from someone else?

    By hardening the bones and strengthening fascia and tendons we make the hand able to withstand contact it would otherwise be damaged by.

Medicinal herbs such as Dit Da Jow aid in this process. Iron Shirt Qi Gong will enable your entire body to withstand blows but Iron Palm specific training will only develop the hands. In Iron Power Palm we focus on the hands as the primary weapon but develop secondary weapons and progress to Iron Shirt also.

- Why does one need Iron palm when one's soft hand can shock the internal organs?

A soft hand can shock the internal organs but an Iron Palm blow may actually rupture them causing serious trauma or death.

- Good Knuckle Conditioning?

    - What the heck are you trying to toughen your knuckles for?

Knuckle conditioning is common in Karate, Wing Tsun, Tae Kwon Do and most martial arts. This enables one to strike harder with a closed fist.

    - What has knuckle conditioning got to do with it?

In Iron Palm for the most part we avoid direct knuckle strikes. This is because too many of these strikes will damage the finger joints which can eventually result in arthritis. Instead we practise mostly the backhand slap. This will strengthen the same bones and tissues as used in a closed fist blow. So the knuckles are conditioned with less risk of injury.

- How are you going to hit hard enough to knock someone down or out with one hit?

    - Is there a way to make your punches more powerful?

Generally it is claimed that Iron Palm will increase the power in ones punches and strikes by a factor of 5 to 10 times.

- Are there any techniques that make your punch ten times more powerful?

With persistent daily practise it should be possible for most beginners to martial arts to achieve this. By combining Iron Palm and western strength training you will be able to increase your striking power by a factor of 5 to 10.

- What should be the effect on an opponent of a sternum shot properly executed?

Do not perform a sternum shot with Iron Palm unless you are in a life or death encounter and must kill the opponent. Any Iron Palm strike to a point like the sternum, carotid, Adams Apple and certain parts of the head can result in death. There are other targets you can use to injure rather than kill. Iron Palm is a deadly skill and must not be used in anger.

- You ever see UFC fighters punch the chest?

UFC and MMA fighters are athletes involved in a sport. They are not fighting to the death. Iron Palm is a military technique developed to kill the opponent in combat. So comparisons must take this into account.

- Makes your bones harder to break?

  - Does anybody know exactly how it makes your bones denser (is there a doctor in the house?)

When the bones are struck micro damage is caused which results in calcification and eventual strengthening of the bone over time. The bone marrow is also stimulated and transformed from fat to blood over time.

- Also how long does it take for the hands to become iron?

The training is broken down thus: 3 months on mung bean bags, 3 months on smooth stone bags, 3 months on steel shot bags, 3 months on steel ball bearing bags. Then train on ball bearings in the future.

So the answer is one year of progressive daily practise.

- Does it make a style/system more superior?

    - Do you agree or disagree with the author of "Model Mugging" that palm heel strikes represent the best way to counter attack your opponent in a street defence situation?

The advantage is that palm strikes normally do not break the hand or damage fingers as fist hits can. In the military Special Forces are often encouraged to use palm rather than fist strikes, as a soldier with finger damage cannot operate a rifle. Palm striking is a more intelligent approach in the long term.

- How to strengthen hands in martial arts?

Many methods are used to strengthen the hands and these are covered in section three of this book.

- Does iron palm training have a use in MMA?

To some extent if you want to knock an opponent out but Iron Palm is a deadly skill that can cause death.

- How to break boards in martial arts?

3 months of the initial level Iron Palm conditioning will enable you to make board breaks.

- Is this preparation necessary?

- Is it necessary to do this to break a single board?

Many people in martial arts such as Karate and Tae Kwon Do perform breaks but in Iron Palm Kung Fu there is an emphasis on safety and internal medicine that these other schools lack. So Iron Palm training is not required to perform breaks but superior breaks can be performed without long-term health damage using Iron Palm rather than the other schools.

- How can you harden yourself for martial arts?

- Is it the same as normal breaks or internal?

Iron Palm employs a balance between internal and external methods. Most other schools use hard external methods only which can result in nerve and joint damage, broken bones and arthritis.

- Is it deadly?

Yes Iron Palm training results in dangerous skills that can cause death and serious injury. Do not use these skills in a sport fight.

- But can it kill someone?

- What is a bottom break?

A bottom break is when the Iron Palm proponent selectively breaks the bottom brick in a stack. This is sometimes called vibrating palm. Some proponents can break any selected slab or brick in a stack. This implies that specific organs or Chi channels can be targeted in an opponent's body.

- What about coconut breaks?

- So what's fake about the coconut break?

Nothing is fake about the coconut break. Coconuts are very hard and brittle and analogous to the human skull. It is assumed that if you can break a swinging coconut you can smash an opponents skull in a standing position. Clearly this is a deadly skill and very dangerous.

- What's a hammer strike?

A hammer strike employs a closed fist striking downward on the edge of the hand.

- Does Wing Chun Train or Use The Iron Palm?

Wing Chun does employ Iron Palm as a section of the training. Most western Wing Chung students are not Iron Palm. Wing Chun uses wooden dummy and wall bag strikes, which will develop Iron Palm and Iron Hand to a certain extent. The Wing Chun dummy & Choy Lee Fut dummy can be used for Iron Palm conditioning and are great for forearm training.

- Kung fu is for multiple opponents isn't it?

Fighting methods that rely on grappling such as BJJ have proven to be the best in MMA bouts but these methods are generally good against a single opponent. Muay Thai, Kung Fu and other methods that focus on striking are more effective against multiple opponents. For this reason a rounded approach is recommended. Learn Both BJJ and Muay Thai in addition to your Kung Fu. When combined with Iron Qi Gong this will make you a very formidable fighter. In you first year focus only on Iron Qi Gong and aerobic *anaerobic conditioning and flexibility. You may like to learn Sanshou in place of Muay Thai.

- How could iron finger work in a fight you ask?

Iron finger is the conditioning required for Chin Na and other grappling methods. Best to investigate Chin Na and Dim Mak for an answer to this question.

- 'Cinnabar Palm' technique?

  Cinnabar palm is an obsolete method of applying poison to the hands, usually mercury. When struck the poison would enter the wound. Clearly in these modern times we don't need to mess with such dangerous things.

- Anyone think this type of training is stupid?

- How many fights are you going to get in in your life?

  Only one incidence of rape or a brutal knife fight could destroy your life for many years. So really its not a question of how many fights will you ever be in. Rather how much do you value your personal security?

- What are your chances of being attacked by someone wearing armour?

  If you are in the military fairly high - if you are a civilian practically nil.

- What is the likelihood of needing to have superbly conditioned knuckles in order to defend yourself?

- Who teaches it?

  Today there are many teachers in the west for Iron Palm. Probably not in your town or city but certainly on the Internet. In coming years Qi Gong and Iron Body methods will become more common in the west. For now these skills will give you a distinct advantage. A simple search online will reveal many courses on the subject. You can also try your local Kung Fu schools for information.

- Should I try to learn it?

- What are the different types of Iron Palm?

Yes there are different types. We have discussed the difference between Chinese and Korean or Japanese methods. Among the Chinese methods there are differences also and I would expect that over time as you master the skill you will develop your own personal method of training.
Examples are Tiger Iron Palm, Shaolin Iron Palm, Vibrating Palm, Internal / External Palm and so on.

- Are there other (proven) benefits of Iron Palm?

Some would argue yes. In fact if you spend many hours each day on Iron Qi Gong you will tend to neglect your cardiovascular and anaerobic training. Iron Palm is a skill to make your strikes more powerful. That is its purpose. You should balance this training with other conditioning. The training will make your bone structure much stronger above and beyond what weight training can achieve.

- How long must you practice?

A minimum of one 30-minute session per day is recommended. You can do 2-3 per day if you have time and can avoid injury.

- The Most Well-conditioned Hands in the Martial Arts World?

There is actually a world breaking association that holds contests to prove who the greatest breakers are. www.usbawba.com is the URL. Go there to check out the world's top breakers, current world records, membership and events.

Current Breaking World Records:

Board Breaking:

> Most 1" Boards broken in 10 seconds - Gary Reho - 126 boards

Most 1" Boards broken in Fifteen Minutes - Fernando Camareno - 1160 boards

Most 1" Boards broken with a single Ridgehand Strike - Paul Hickey - 6 boards

Most 1" Boards broken in One Minute - Leif Becker - 487 boards

Concrete Breaking:

Most 2" Concrete Patio Blocks broken in 10 seconds - Larry Fields - 113 blocks

Most Concrete Tiles broken in One Minute - Fernando Camareno - 468 tiles

Other Breaking and Sanctioned Records:

Most Coconuts broken in 20 seconds - Ralph Bergamo - 9 coconuts

Most Rebar bent with Throat in 30 Seconds - Fernando Camareno - 33 rebar

2. Training

- How long does it take to become proficient?

A basic level is achieved in 3 months. After a year of daily practise you will have mastered Iron Palm and can work on increasing your power.

- Train from Books & Videos or an Instructor?

- Could you point out a book/video on this?

Well you have the book in your hands. I also recommend Ultimate Iron Palm from Sifu Wing Lam. There are several Iron Palm video courses available. If you want to break coconuts James Lacey is the expert at www.IronPalm.com. Richard Clear also offers internal Iron Palm training on his website and info on applying Iron Palm for one hit knockdowns. I also have found Wing Chun wall bag and wooden dummy videos to be helpful.

- Perhaps a website with a graphical description of this?

I recommend youtube if you want a demonstration of breaks. This is the clearest graphical information.

- Does anyone know any sites or books I can buy on bone conditioning?

- What experience do you have?

I have practised Iron Palm and Iron shirt while in the military many years ago and recently decided to take it up permanently as preliminary self defence conditioning.

- What does your system aim to achieve?

Iron Power Palm aims to condition your hands to deliver lethal strikes. Other striking parts of the body are conditioned and this in turn leads into Iron Shirt defensive conditioning.

- Could you describe what it consists of?

A progressive conditioning program involving a number of exercises practised daily using inexpensive equipment.

- Why are you trying something you saw out of a magazine?

Iron Palm breaks should only be practised after a substantial conditioning period of 3 months. Even then the initial breaking should be done gradually to ensure safety.

- Why would anyone in their right mind want to hit themselves to acquire the iron body?

Iron Body training is not painful although it certainly looks like it must be. Done properly there in no damage done to the body. The training enables one to withstand blows with a blunt instrument or body part and some weapons.

- Safety

- What is the safest way to do it?

The safe way is a slow and gradual progression. Do not strike the bags with anything near full force. Progress from mung beans to small stones to iron shot to steel ball bearings with 3 months minimum on each.

- Are these methods all really safe?

No method is truly safe. There is always a possibility of injury and tissue damage in martial arts training. With Iron Palm our goal is to minimize the risks involved. We do this by always massaging the hands with proper liniment and progressive training.

- Are there any fraudulent methods that I should be aware of?

As in all things there are fraudulent methods. Basically the proof is in the results. If a method produces breaks but also injury this is not what we call Iron Palm. If a method has a false lineage but produces results without injury then the lineage is irrelevant. More important is the quality of Dit Da Jow and I suspect there may be some false and suspect brands of Jow being sold online.

- Is there any safe way to develop it?

That's what Iron Palm training is all about.

- How can knuckle push-ups be bad?

Knuckle push ups like fist strikes when over used can damage the finger joints and cause arthritis. Backhand slapping is a safer way to train.

- How do you know you are doing it correctly?

Iron Palm training is actually very simple. If you watch videos, read and have a few lessons that should be all you need to master the techniques with some dedication and time. Iron Palm is not rocket science it simply requires discipline.

- Is Iron Palm dangerous for you?

There are claims Iron Palm causes heart disease and impotence. The impotence claims arise from certain Jow that is toxic. If you refrain from using toxic jow you can not have this problem. While training Iron Qi Gong it is easy to neglect other aspects of training such as cardio vascular fitness. A simple solution is to get some Kettlebells and follow the "Viking Warrior Conditioning" book. Training in other aspects of Qi Gong will teach you to control Qi in your heart meridian and to balance the Qi.

- When is it safe age to practice iron palm?

Generally in the later adolescent years from 19 or so it is safe to begin Iron Palm training.

- Are there long-term damages like increased risk of arthritis?

Yes if progression, proper form and massage are not used. Also if injured one must break from training until fully healed. By using diligent healing methods long-term injury should be avoidable.

- What kind of exercises can I do to build my iron palm?

There are five basic Iron Palm strikes used on the flat bag. Palm slap, knife hand strike, back hand slap, grab with fingertips and palm heel strike.

- Is he slapping it?

Slapping is the primary Iron Palm strike.

- How many times a day do you need to do this for optimal results?

One to three half hour sessions per day.

- How many days a week?

Seven days per week is recommended.

- What about after 90 days?

After 90 days a harder substance is placed in the bag. Training frequency does not change.

- How many reps should I do in a set?

Just train at a steady relaxed pace for the allocated time. Never hit with full force. It is a gradual process that takes time. Don't bother to count reps this will make you lose focus.

- Can you wear gloves while doing this training and still improve your punching power?

Gloves are not required for the bag as it has a canvas cover but may be a good idea for bucket thrusting.

- But what exactly is wrong with wearing gloves?

Gloves are not required and may negate the training by making the surface too soft.

- Why wear them?

People can wear gloves to prevent the skin from rupturing during real breaks and to protect the finger tips during thrusting training.

- Is the training for iron palm the same as iron fist in regards to the strengthen of the hands?

Yes many of the methods are the same. Iron Palm training generally will result in Iron Fist.

- How to go about Iron fist training?

The best way is to first develop Iron Palm then go on to Wing Tsun wall bag training. Then you will have both Iron Palm and Fist.

- What is the right way to align your knuckles when punching the bags?
- What exactly is the "proper" way to punch and the proper bone alignment?
- What's the correct way to punch?
- How do you aim it?
- How do you execute it properly?
- How do you train it?

The UK wing chun association UKWCKFA has a great video on wall bag training that covers closed fist knuckle punching I recommend this resource for all of your questions on this topic. Basically the two knuckles closest to the thumb are the strongest structurally. So while all of the knuckles can benefit from conditioning it is these two that are traditionally conditioned for striking. Watching the wall bag training video will clear all of these questions up for you. In strict Iron Palm we minimize the use of direct knuckle blows.

- Can you punch as hard as you do with gloves on?

A trained Iron Palm expert can punch harder and cause more damage without gloves. This is because the bones and ligaments sustain minimal damage. Gloves may be practical to avoid cutting the skin.

- What is it they do to harden they knuckles an can anyone explain the whole process?

Karate students use the Makiwara, closed fist press-ups and knuckle blows on hard surfaces to form calluses on the knuckles. This training can eventually cause arthritis and disfigurement, which is not our goal with Iron Palm.

- What is the optimal number of punches to throw at the bags?

Rather than counting punches it is best to set a time limit for the training session and simply sustain a steady relaxed pace while concentrating on the strikes.

- But at what stage of your training should one practise "the one inch punch"?

The one-inch punch is part of Wing Chun Kung Fu not Iron Palm. You had best consult an appropriate sifu for an answer.

- Are boxers punches hard bare knuckled?

Most boxers may have considerable striking power from bag work but will lack the structural adaptation the Iron Palm training develops. So a boxer performing an equal strike may damage his hands when an Iron Palm master would not. The same goes for weight lifters and strength athletes.

- How can I make my fists harder?

Iron Palm conditioning is the best way.

- Will your knuckles adapt to hitting hard stuff?

Yes but it is not advised without great care.

- Any suggestions for Iron Palm / Iron Bone training?

Follow the program in Part One of Iron Power Palm for Iron Palm conditioning. For general Iron Bone and Iron Body training there are some very good books and videos available now for both internal and external methods. A high level can be attained with one year of dedication.

- Are there any different ways to practice iron palm?

Yes there are several popular methods for Iron Palm. We use the shaolin method as a basis in Iron Power Palm but I encourage you to explore as many methods as possible for a well rounded education. By combining methods and thinking of new ideas you may develop a superior system that others can learn.

- What martial arts should I take?

I recommend in addition to Qi Gong, BJJ, Muay Thai and various Kung Fu methods including Wing Tsun, Chin Na and Dim Mak.

- How long must you practice

A minimum of one half hour daily for one year to achieve mastery with ongoing training there after.

- Can older people train their bodies to stretch like a gymnast?

Largely yes. It is actually the nervous system that determines flexibility in the absence of joint damage so age is not restrictive.

- How does one get an "Iron body"?

By training in Iron Shirt and Iron Qi Gong.

3. Chi

- Does chi pass through all the bricks?

Chi in the body generally refers to electromagnetic energy. It can also refer to kinetic and other forms of energy. Clearly kinetic energy is transferred through the bricks.

- Shouldn't Chi be developed before external methods?

Yes it is preferred that internal Qi Gong is studied and developed to some extent so Chi can be utilized in the Iron Palm practise and protect the body from damage.

- May I recommend some qigong that will focus your qi in your hands?

There are several internal Iron Palm courses available. Richard Clear, James Lacey and Thomas Keen offer video training and I'm sure there are many Chinese language courses where Iron Palm is very common.

- Internal shaolin?

- Isn't Iron Shirt part of marrow/brain washing?

Yes it is but specific to the hands. Largely the same procedure is used.

- 18 Daoist palms?

This is James Lacey's school which is largely dedicated to specialized

Iron Palm for breaking coconuts. They offer Dit Da Jow and many training videos.

4. Equipment

- What do people use for this training?

Canvas bags filled with dry beans, round gravel, steel shot and steel ball bearings. Wooden and steel rollers for the fore arms. Wing Chun wooden dummy and wall bags. If Iron body is done then various instruments for beating and massaging the body are used also. Most of the equipment is very inexpensive and easy to buy or make. Standard and specialized western gym equipment is used to build strength in the hands and arms.

- 3 section wall bag - any safety issues?

The only issue is possible damage to the knuckles.

- Iron Arm Roller

    - Do I use the rolling pin first and then the dit da jow?

Really its best to massage with Jow before, during and after the sessions.

    - Where can you get a rolling pin?

A roller is easy to make from round fence post or similar. Later on a heavy length of steel pipe or rod can be used.

    - Roller Bar

    - Think escrima sticks will do the trick of the roller bar?

No because the bar must be heavy.

- What kind of tape should you tape up the rolling bar with?

Taping the bar is not required but if you must ordinary duct tape will do the job.

- Anyone here use something else to hit their arms with other than a human partner?

Special long bags are available for hitting body parts. Arms can also be trained on posts, tree's etc. Later steel bar can be used on the arms.

- Why use a bag of beans?
  - is there an adequate replacement for mung bean ?

Soya beans, chick peas etc can replace the mung bean if you cant find any.

- Where can I buy mung beans for iron palm?

Try your local Asian super market. I got chickpeas for my first bag.

- Could I use rice instead of beans in my iron palm bag?

Rice grains are too small. Try beans instead. Iron Palm is all about strengthening the bones and fascia. This takes too long with sand and rice.

- Wood and concrete for other purposes then to break?

Yes you can train directly on these surfaces once you have twelve months of daily conditioning.

- How do I make a wooden dummy?

A simple search on Google will reveal many plans for making a wooden dummy. To buy such a dummy can cost between $600 and $1500 so building your own is appealing.

I have an even better suggestion that makes the job much easier. Make your dummy from steel. Buy a 5-6 ft length of steel pipe from a scrap yard. Have the leg and arms welded on at your local engineering school for cheap. Such a dummy should only cost $200 or so and be superior to a wooden one. I don't provide plans here – just check on the internet. Coat the final product with hammerite paint.

Parts:

> Base plate
> Post steel tube
> 3 x arm
> 1 x leg

5. Dit Da Jow

- Which is Best?

- What is the background of the person and their formula(s)?

    There are many Dit Da Jow suppliers online these days. This was not the case ten years ago. Some are distributed by large-scale operations in China *while others a re back yard operations in western countries. Investigate the company online before you buy and check ebay for a good price.

- How is the liniment made (there are many ways)?

    The liniment is made from a special selection of herbs soaked for several months in alcohol.

- But also what type of substrate are the herbs soaked in?

Rice wine is the favoured alcohol. Vodka and similar can be substituted. Don't use denatured alcohols as these will dry out the skin.

- Is it pure or is the liniment diluted?

The liniment should not be diluted in any way.

- Are they all the best?

You will need to investigate the various jows for the most suitable. Different jows have been created for different levels of training and different striking surfaces.

- Do they really understand how to use hit medicine as it relates to martial arts training?

Dit Da Jow is intended as a massage liniment and the massage of hands must be completed for a considerable duration. There is the temptation to be lazy and apply a little Jow for a short massage each day. Really liberal amounts of Jow must be used and the massage continued for as long as the beating. You will find that this really pays off.

- Are there other products that act like Dit Da Jow?

No. Dit Da Jow has taken 1000 years to evolve along with Iron Palm training. There is presently no other comparable medicine.

- Where to buy it?

- Can someone give me some links to sites where I can get some good medicine?

Some of these sell pre-made Jow, others the herbs.

www.Ebay.com

www.Amazon.com
www.IronPalm.com
www.TheIronlotusSociety.com
www.seaofchi.com/tlu.html
www.plumdragonherbs.com
www.scarfamilyditdajow.com
www.shenmartialarts.com
www.coilingdragon.com
www.eastearthtrade.com
www.orientalherb.com

- Do you use the supermarket brands or does your school sell you dit da jow?

Personally I combine two different commercial Chinese brands having researched the ingredients.

- Does anyone know a place where I can order dit da jow ingredients that is reliable?

The websites listed above should be able to supply quality Jow.

- Where is the best place to get a reliable recipe for Dit Da Jow?

www.IronPalm.com has useful information on Dit Da Jow recipes. Here are some sample jow recipes:

Recipe 1

- 1 bottle of strong vodka, gin or Chinese rice wine
- Artemesia (Liu ji nu) - 5g
- Borneol (Bingpian) - 1g
- Carthamus (Honghua) - 5geastearthtrade.com
- Catechu (Ercha) - 8g
- Cinnabar (Zhusha) - 5g
- Cirsium (DaJi) - 1g

- Dragon's Blood (Xuejie) - 30g
- Mastic (Ruxiang) - 5g /www.orientalherb.com
- Musk (Shexiang) - 1g
- Myrrh (Moyao) - 5g
- Pinellia (ShengBanXia) - 5g

Recipe 2

- Arnica blossoms (anti-inflammatory, pain relief)
- Comfrey (anti-inflammatory, pain relief)
- Blessed Thistle (blood purifier) eastearthtrade.com
- Goldenseal root (antibiotic, wound healing)
- Ginger root (circulation, wound healing, pain relief)
- Myrrh (antiseptic, circulation, wound healing)
- Sasparilla root (blood purifier)
- Witch Hazel (anti-inflammatory, pain relief)

Recipe 3

- Alcohol (Vodka, Gin, Brandy - even Rubbing Alcohol) 1 or 2 quarts
- Breadstraw
- Calendula (Marigold)
- Camomile
- Comfrey (if you can still get it - you may have to grow your own if you want to add this)
- Common Club Moss
- Cowslip
- Dandelion
- Shepherd's Purse
- Stinging Nettle
- St. John's Wort
- Wintergreen oil

Recipe 4

- Alcohol (Vodka, Gin, Brandy - even Rubbing Alcohol) 1 or 2 quarts
- Breadstraw
- Horsetail
- Mallow
- Cow parsnip
- Fenugreek
- Walnut
- Yellow Dead Nettle
- Calendula (Marigold)
- Camomile
- Comfrey
- Common Club Moss
- Cow slip
- Dandelion
- Shepherd's Purse
- Stinging Nettle
- St. John's Wort
- Wintergreen oil

Recipe 5 (oriental herb company formula)

- Alcohol
- Water
- Arnica
- Camphor
- Rhizoma Rhei
- Myrrh
- Frankincense
- Asarum
- Polygala
- Angelica Dahurica
- Arisaema
- Pinellia
- Achyranthes
- Ledbouriella Sesloides

- Sanguis Draconis
- Rehmannia
- Angelica Sinensis
- Notopteryguim
- Brassica Alba
- Drynaria Fortunei
- Dipsacus
- Pseudoginseng
- Acanthopanax
- Angelica Pubescens
- Gardenia
- Pyrolusite
- Lycopodium
- Carthamus
- Ligusticum
- Ziziphus
- Sparganium

Recipe 6 (Shen Bao Tien Chi & Analgesic Yao Jin)

- Radix Notoginseng 30%
- Daemonorops Draco 10%
- Radix Zanthoxyli 20%
- Radix Cudraniae 8%
- Herba Gendarussae 8%
- Hydnocarpus Anthelmintica Pier 8%
- Red Cortex Eucommiae 8%
- Caulis Entadae 8%

Recipe 7 (Five Photos Brand)

- Cattail pollen
- Peony (red)
- Dang gui (Angelica sinensis)
- Dragon's blood
- Frankincense

- Myrrh
- Peppermint
- Safflower
- Tienchi
- Water

There are many more on the net. Some popular commercial Jows have the ingredients listed. Try asking at your Chinese herbal store also.

- Do you use the same herbs as other Iron Palm experts?

Some herbs are common in a large number of Jows but others are dissimilar. You may choose to become an expert on herbs or you may simply choose to trust the experience of others. Certainly Chinese herbal medicine is a complicated subject when the effects upon chi are taken into account.

- For how long did you soak hands?

The hands should not just be soaked but massaged. Preferably for an equal duration to that of the training session.

- Was the medicine hot or cold?

There is no need to heat the liniment.

- How long should I wait before I can wash my hands when using dit da jow after iron palm practice?

Its up to you but the longer you can leave it on the better.

- Do you apply iron palm liniment on your knuckles before and after you do this training?

Yes the entire hand should be deeply massaged with the liniment.

- Do you have a recommendation for a commercially available jow or do you always make your own?

  - Tiger balm?

Tiger balm is not a Dit Da Jow and is no substitute for it.

- How & Why Does it work?

Three primary groups of herbs are used. Anti Inflammatory that inhibit rheumatism, Herbs that stop bleeding and herbs that encourage circulation of chi and blood.

  - What type of alcohol to use?

High proof rice wine is preferred.

  - Should vodka be used?

Vodka and other distilled alcohols can be used.

  - Do you feel there is a big difference between using the Chinese wine and neutral grain spirits?

Chinese wine is the traditional ingredient, some other alcohols are equally adequate but some are not.

Iron Hitting Wine Recipe

> Camphor (crushed) 10g
> Raw Fruit of Cape Jasmine 5g
> Raw Root of Kusenoff Monkshood 25g
> Raw Aconite Root 25g
> Raw Tuber Of Jackinthepulpit 25g
> Raw Pinellia Tuber 25g
> Cattail Pollen 25g

Raw Chinese Quince 200g
Raw Rhubarb 150g
Root-Bark of slenderstyle acanthopanax 100g
Rhizome of incised notopterygium 200g
Root of double teeth pubescent angelica 200g
Root of Red Peony 150g

Place in a sealed jar with white wine (Gao Liang Wine or any other high alcohol content wine) for 7-15 days. It can be used for all injuries that don't break the skin.

- I wonder what sort of proof levels Chinese wine comes in?

Chinese wines can be generally classified into two types, namely yellow liquors (huangjiu) or clear (white) liquors (baijiu). Chinese yellow liquors are fermented wines that are brewed directly from grains such as rice or wheat. Such liquors contain less than 20% alcohol, due to the inhibition of fermentation by ethanol at this concentration. These wines are traditionally pasteurised, aged, and filtered before their final bottling for sale to consumers. Yellow liquors can also be distilled to produce white liquors, or baijiu (see below). White liquors (baijiu) are also commonly called shaojiu, which means "hot liquor" or "burned liquor", either because of the burning sensation in the mouth during consumption, the fact that they are usually warmed before being consumed, or because of the heating required for distillation. Liquors of this type typically contain more than 30% alcohol in volume since they have undergone distillation. There are a great many varieties of distilled liquors, both unflavoured and flavoured.

Fen jiu - this wine was dated back to Northern and Southern Dynasties (550 A.D.). It is the original Chinese white wine made from sorghum. Alcohol content by volume: 63-65%.

Zhu Ye Qing jiu - this wine is Fen jiu brewed with a dozen or more of selected Chinese herbal medicine. One of the ingredients is bamboo leaves which gives the wine a greenish colour and its name. Alcohol content by volume: 46%.

Mao Tai jiu - this wine has a production history of over 200 years. It is named after its origin at Mao Tai town in Guizhou Province. It is make from wheat and sorghum with a unique distilling process that involves seven iterations of the brewing cycle. This wine is made famous to the western world when the Chinese government served this in state banquets entertaining the US presidents. Alcohol content by volume: 54-55%.

Gao Liang jiu - Goa Liang is the Chinese name for sorghum. Besides sorghum, the brewing process also use barley, wheat etc. The wine was originated from DaZhiGu since the Ming Dynasty. Nowadays, Taiwan is a large producer of gao liang jiu. Alcohol content by volume: 61-63%. Mei Gui Lu jiu (rose essence wine) - a variety of gao liang jiu with distil from a special species of rose and crystal sugar. Alcohol content by volume: 54-55%.

Wu Jia Pi jiu - a variety of gao liang jiu with a unique selection of Chinese herbal medicine added to the brew. Alcohol content by volume: 54-55%.

Da Gu jiu - Originate from Sichuan with 300 year of history. This wine is made of sorghum and wheat by fermenting in a unique process for a long period in the cellar. Alcohol content by volume: 52%.

Yuk Bing Shiu jiu - a rice wine with over 100 year history. It is made of steamed rice. It is stored a long period after distillation. Alcohol content by volume: 30%.

Sheung Jing (double distil) and San Jing (triple distil) Jiu - two varieties of rice wine by distilling twice and three times respectively. Alcohol content by volume: 32% and 38-39% respectively.

San Hua (three flowers) jiu - a rice wine made in Guilin with allegedly over a thousand year history. It is famous for the fragrant herbal addition and the use of spring water from Mount Elephant in the region. Alcohol content by volume: 55-57%.

Fujian Glutinous Rice wine - made by adding a long list of expensive Chinese herbal medicine to glutinous rice and a low alcohol rice wine distil. The unique brewing technique use another wine as raw material, not starting with water. The wine has an orange red colour. Alcohol content by volume: 18%.

Hua Diao jiu - a variety of yellow wine originates from Shaoxing, Zhejiang. It is made of glutinous rice and wheat. Alcohol content by volume: 16%.

- Wouldn't you say that crushing up "certain" ingredients allow it to dissolve in the mix faster than leaving it in a big hard lump of mineral etc?

General practise is to crush the herbs. Note that some herbs require water rather than alcohol to extract the medicine.

- What internal medicines can you recommend?

Internal medicine known as "hit pills" are simple to make. They can be used for most general and traumatic injuries, including: bruising, sprains, tears and fractures of tendon, muscle, ligaments, bone and skin.

Honey (Feng Mi): 4.0 g.
Angelica Root (Dang Gui): 3.0 g.
Pseudoginseng root (San-Qi): 3.0 g.
Carthamus flower (Hong Hua): 2.0 g
Cattail [Typha] pollen (Pu Huang): 2.0 g.
Cistanche stem (Rou Cong Rong): 2.0 g.
Polygonum root (He Shou Wu): 2.0 g.
Ammomum fruit seeds (Sha ren): 1.0 g.

Dipsacus root (Xu Duan): 1.0 g.
Dragon's Blood [Daemonorops] resin (Xue Jie): 1.0 g.
Frankincense Gum resin (Ru Xiang): 1.0 g.
Myrryh Gum resin (Mo Yao): 1.0 g.
Paeonia root "red" (Chi Shao): 1.0 g.
Curcuma rhizome (Tu Si Zi): 0.5 g.
Rhubarb [Rheum] rhizome (Da Huang): 0.5 g.

You may use additional items such as common joint supplements. I recommend western nutritional joint support supplements such as Glucosamine, Chronodroitin, Green Lipped Mussel extract and omega 3. You can try Cissus too.

This prescription is for a single standard 25 gram dose, made into two rolled pills. Adjust the list to match the amount required.

A standard daily dose is one to four, single standard doses, each day. The normal dose is one or two pills three times a day.

Simply grind all of the components together. First combine resins, gums and sticky things together and grind them smooth. Add other ground items like the cattail pollen and re-grind. Then knead the other ground items together, into the mixture. So its kind of like dough. When the kneaded mixture looks uniform, roll the dough into a uniform rope. If you have problems keeping the rope together add a little more honey and re-kneed and re-roll the rope. Cut a small length from the rope and weigh it, gauge the size for the weight, look for a weight of 12 or 13 grams each.

Roll each segment into uniform balls. Wrap each ball into a square of wax paper; twist each of the four corners together. You should have what looks like a "cherry bomb."

Dip each into melted wax, to seal and protect the pills. The honey is a preservative and a binding agent for the pills, as well as a wound healer, as an ingredient.

If this is too much work, expensive various simpler versions of this prescription are available in the Chinese Herb stores, as pre-made pills. Five Photos Brand is a Chinese supplier that makes internal bruise medicine as well as external Jow. They are a trusted and common supplier.

Lung Choy Shung Medicine Factory Hong Kong, China: Five Photos Brand, Tien Ta Wan.
United Pharmaceutical Manufacturer Kwangchow, China: Yang Cheng Brand, Tieh Ta Wan.
Shanghai Chinese Medicine Works, China: Restorative Brand, Ren Shen Zai Zao Wan.
United Pharmaceutical Manufacturer; Guangzhou, Guangdong, China: Hsiung Tan Tieh Ta Wan.

Note: You can chew these, or cut them up into smaller bits to make eating easier, or dissolve the dose into a cup of hot water or tea. You can also mix these with wine or alcohol and use them for external injuries as well!

The wax covering needs to be removed before using. It is only to protect the pills for storage!
Five Photos Brand is a Chinese supplier that makes internal bruise medicine as well as external Jow. They are a trusted and common supplier.

I also recommend the following nutritional joint support supplements:

Glucosamine

> Glucosamine occurs naturally in the body in the joints. It is made from glucose and glutamine. This is a very popular supplement for joints.

Chronodroitin

> Chronodroitin is often included with glucosamine in supplement capsules. Chronodroitin is found in cartilage. Studies show significant improvement in pain and inflammation and improved joint function when the two supplements are used together.

Green Lipped Mussel extract

> Perna canaliculus, Green-lipped mussel is a New Zealand shellfish, the extract of which has been shown to be useful in the treatment of osteoarthritis, rheumatoid Arthritis, bursitis, skin inflammation, Connective Tissue Repair and sports related injuries.

Omega 3

> Omega-3 fatty acids are considered essential fatty acids meaning the body can not make them and they must be ingested.

Cissus Quadrangularus

> This is an Indian herb used in ayurvedic medicine. I am giving it a special mention as many martial artists are unfamiliar with it although it is quite common in bodybuilding. Cissus quadrangularus is known to strengthen bone and assist with fracture healing. For this reason it is of special interest to those of us doing Iron Palm, which causes micro fractures and bone stress. Cissus is also commonly used by people with joint and connective tissue problems and has many strongly positive reviews. Cissus also lowers cholesterol. USPlabs Super Cissus RX is the most highly recommended product at the time of writing. It is available in capsules or in one kilo powder packages.

- Is it really safe for everyone to take the internal dit da jow?

Possibly not and a medical practitioner should be consulted before taking internal medicine.

- Do you have to follow a special diet when using the internal jow?

This is often the case and internal medicines are also often formulated for the individual. For this reason you must consult with a Chinese physician for advice on diet.

- What are the ingredients in it used for and how does it help in the whole process of practicing iron palm?

Internal medicines often contain many of the same ingredients as external but in smaller amounts. Longer lasting injuries and internal bruising may require internal medicines.

- Why do you use certain things in the jow?

The properties of Jow and its classes of ingredient have been discussed.

- Should I make my own?

You may wish to experiment with different formulas. In this case making your own is the only way.

- Injury

- Are you bruising?

Small point impact bruises are common with Iron Palm training. With Jow and massage they tend to heal overnight. If untreated these can lead to nerve damage or joint problems depending upon the location.

- What do you think happens when you bruise?

Bruising is the rupture of internal blood vessels that results in stagnation of blood and an accumulation of waste material.

- Does the skin matter so much?

In Iron Palm we avoid the formation of calluses for the most part. Strength training associated with the Iron Palm can result in callous formation.

- Calluses?

- Do you need callous to hit someone in the solar plexus?

No calluses are not required.

- Is that callus going to make a difference?

If you have trained by the Iron Palm method having calluses will offer you no advantage at all.

- Joint pain?

    Joint pain can occur when the hands strike on the improper locations repeatedly. This often happens by accident during training.

- Sore muscles?

    Generally Iron Palm will not cause muscular pain during the striking training. Strength training can however cause pain periodically.

- How to get the swelling down?

    If you have swelling from bruises use R.I.C.E rest, ice, compression, elevation - also massage with Jow and possibly try internal medicine.

- How do you harden/toughen your tendons to prevent injury?

    This is part of the process in Iron Qi Gong.

- How do you move tendons away from your knuckles to be able to harden your knuckles?

The tendons are not required to move anywhere. What will happen is that the tendons and fascia will become stronger and more resistant to stress and blows.

- Toxicity

- How do you do iron palm training without becoming infertile?

  Some advanced formulas of Jow can apparently cause this if used for several years.

- I want to have very conditioned hands that will do well in combat without taking the stuff to make you infertile can anybody give an answer?

  The vast majority of Jow formulas do not cause infertility. So really this is not a problem if you discuss your Jow with a Chinese medicine expert.

- How necessary is Dit Da Jow to Iron Fist/Palm training?

  The use of Jow is considered to be essential for Iron Palm practise.

6. Additional Questions

1. When one is training in Tai Chi Chuan, can one take up the Iron Palm at the same time?

   Many Sifu's will tell you outright that this is not advantageous. They will also prevent you from doing weight training or cardio training. I tend to disagree with this. Many of these Sifu's have a vested interest in promoting their particular style or methods.

   Rather than denying a student the benefits of various forms of training I feel it is better to find a solution that allows maximum development of all martial and fitness skills.

This will require recuperation and periodization so your body is recovered from the strength gong and iron gong before you perform your Chi training. In this way the training remains harmonious. You must research recuperation methods and cycle your training accordingly. Do not blindly follow the advice of any Sifu but seek wisdom.

2. Of the two recommended methods for training, which is the faster one, the use of peas or the use of iron filings?

The use of steel shot is more affective clearly but it is best to gradually condition in stages, so use the mung beans for some weeks then progress.

3. If a morning and evening session is devoted daily to training, how long would it take to be able to break bricks?

With two diligent sessions per day it should then only take 50 days. With 3 sessions 30 days.

4. Is it sufficient if only the right hand alone is used in training?

It is not uncommon for people to train a single hand, particularly with the direct method that can be injurious. From a practical perspective, if you are using safe and proper Iron Palm technique it makes sense to train both hands equally.

5. If your training methods are adhered to, and success is acquired, are there further methods of training?

Yes, one can progress to advanced internal methods of training that are not explained in this book.

6. If iron filings are not obtainable, would ball bearings serve as a substitute?

Bearing balls are the next step after steel shot. They are larger and will result in point bruising if preliminary training on beans, stones and steel shot has not been completed.

7. Why must one put on a mask when training?

    The purpose of a mask is to filter off any dust that might be inspired into one's system.

    Obviously you don't have to wear a mask but if iron dust is inhaled regularly you can develop serious poisoning from this. The only treatment for Iron poisoning is venesection.

8. Is it fitting to train the Iron Palm and the Kung-Fu at the same time?

    Yes. Both methods of training at the same time are not contradictory.

9. After what duration of time call one take his meal following a training session?

    Usually its best to wait an hour or so. Different people have different tolerances. A light meal prior to training will prevent hunger, which is a distraction.

10. Why is it that after a full year's training, I am still incapable of breaking a brick?

    You may have trained incorrectly, you may be striking the brick incorrectly or you may simply need to be persistent and spend more time attempting to break while perfecting your method. If the brick does not break this does not mean you have failed. It simply means you must continue to practise breaking the bricks.

11. Is it possible to dispense with the use of medication during training?

    If the wrong medication is applied or if applied in the wrong manner, injury and occasional death could result. Always use Dit Da Jow and internal medicine to protect your joints and fascia.

12. It has been claimed that training in the Iron palm would so roughened the hands, that even one's writing ability would be affected. Is this true?

    If you use the hard external methods this is true but in this book we do not encourage the use of those methods. With the soft methods no sign of training will be visible.

13. How could it be accounted that the 'gentler method' is so effective in training?

    Chi can achieve more than brute strength. It seems counterintuitive but it is true when we see a strong weightlifter or athlete fail to break an object that is simple for an Iron Palm.

    The strength of the Iron Palm is concentrated in the hands.

14. How do you apply medication during training?

    Apply before, after and during the training sessions. Massage it deep into the tissue.

15. Is it true that training for the Iron Palm is only limited to those who possess strength and a good physique?

    No, anybody can complete the training so long as they possess hand and heart health.

16. If your methods are followed which portion of the hand could develop 'Chin', the palms or the fingers?

    When success is achieved, the fingers, palm. wrist and back of the hand would all possess 'Chin'.

17. I have seen people breaking stones weighing from 70 to 80 kilo's with their bare hands? If your instructions are followed, could I expect to achieve the same feat as these people after a hundred days?

    The answer is in the no. It is not possible to achieve the feat of these breakers in a hundred days. What can be achieved in a hundred days, is the ability to break a few bricks.

18. Is it true that three full years is required to achieve such feat?

    If his art is in all probability a true art then it is quite true that it requires three full years of training to achieve such skill.

19. If peas are used for training instead of iron filings, is it still necessary to use medicants?
    Yes. The application of medicants is to aid the circulation in the limbs and to minimise the formation of bruises. Medication, therefore, is necessary irrespective of whether peas or iron filings are used.

20. Who originated the Iron Palm?

    As mentioned in the text, the only historical evidence of the Iron Palm is recorded in the "Yi Chin Ching." The originator is unknown.

21. What benefit is there to the body in training for the Iron Palm?

    The benefit derived from such training, is only limited to the development of 'Chin' in the palm, wrist and forearm. There is no physical fitness benefit other than strengthening of bones and fascia.

22. If there is a wound in the skin, is it advisable to apply medicants under such circumstances?

    No. It is better to wait till the wound is healed. Dit Da Jow liniments can cause infection if applied to open wounds.

23. Is it necessary to warm the 'medicated wine' before application?

    No. It is not necessary.

24. Could ordinary wine be used instead of medicated wine?

    No. The use of ordinary wine cannot be recommended.

25. Is it true that during the hundred days of training, sex is taboo? Is it also true that nocturnal emission, is harmful during training?

    According to my personal opinion it is not recommended to stop sex during the hundred days of training. Like over-eating, too much sex is generally not good but, this does not mean that temperance in sex, is disallowed during training.

Section 3: Hand & Forearm Strength for Martial Artists

Introduction

WELCOME to the world of grip and hand strength training. It's a world with its own culture, terminology and community not to mention history. There are of course many professions that will develop your grip. Tying steel, chopping timber, bricklaying to name but a few will develop a superior grip and if you choose to do some steel or chopping work to enhance your training then kudos to your initiative.

In this section we will examine the means to develop grip and forearm strength athletically. You will be surprised at the vast array of equipment developed for the task and once you begin using this gear you will reflect upon the hand strength of some athletes with awe such as the ability the close over 400 lbs with a hand gripper. All of this grip training will assist immensely with your Iron Palm conditioning.

Everything is covered from anatomy and injury to various routines and in depth discussion of exercises.

You will find your strength can develop quickly and this in turn flows to other strength training using the hands. Many regular people can use additional grip strength, as can many athletes such as martial artists, climbers, golfers, archers and many more.

Once a powerful grip is established the strength athlete can progress along the chain strengthening the upper arms, shoulders, chest, back and legs. Most people neglect grip strength to the detriment of all other athletic development. As a martial artist grip and forearm strength are essential.

Training Principles

Off the top of my head I can think of fifty different weight training principles but here we will discuss only a few of most significance to the training of grip and forearm strength. These will be applied later when you have learned the exercises and are using them in routines.

Its important to note that the Iron Palm training we discussed in earlier sections IS NOT strength training so these principles DO NOT apply to the iron qigong workouts. Only some of the Kung Fu methods are aimed at strength.

Intensity Training

High Intensity Training involves low volume that is low sets and reps with very high resistance. This form of training is suited to natural drug free athletes and hard gainers. High Intensity Training does not sacrifice muscle for the sake of burning fat as high volume weights and traditional cardio can.

High Intensity Training takes many shapes and forms. There is High Intensity Interval Training, which is a very effective fat burning technique. Power conditioning for power lifters often involves very low reps at extreme intensity resulting in strength gains. There is Nautilus machine training invented by Arthur Jones and there is even an exercise machine priced at $14,000 designed specifically for HIIT. Great bodybuilders like Clarence Bass, Casey Viator, Mike Mentzer and Dorian Yates all have followed High Intensity regimes.

High Intensity Training can be implemented for both strength/mass and fat loss/cardio goals simultaneously. Studies have shown High Intensity Interval Training to be far more effective than traditional cardio at burning fat while increasing muscle mass at the same time. This is because the metabolism is stimulated to burn fat at rest.

Studies have shown that the maximum anabolic hormone response peaks at around 45 minutes of exercise and decreases after 90 or so minutes. Training beyond this for natural athletes can be catabolic. Athletes using drugs such as steroids and other types have a greater resistance to catabolic physiology. Their hormones are also being regulated and elevated unnaturally by the drugs. So these people can endure and benefit from volume training that would be catabolic for them under normal circumstances. A high volume cycle may be advantageous to these athletes after the steroid cycle.

This brings us to another possibility – that of cycling high intensity and high volume training regimens.

High Intensity Training hits the fast twitch fibres primarily. It is anaerobic in that glycogen not oxygen is not the primary energy source, despite this it is still an effective means of developing cardiovascular fitness and more effective than high endurance aerobics at burning fat. It also primarily stimulates the fast twitch muscle fibres.

Volume training primarily stimulates the slower twitch muscle fibres and develops muscular endurance. For aerobics training it promotes vascularity, endurance and fat loss. Using both forms of training should theoretically stimulate greater muscle adaptation (endurance / strength) and hypertrophy than using one single regimen alone. Ideally you should strive to develop volume and intensity.

Recovery is one of the key factors in high intensity training. As intensity in your workouts increases over time so your requirement for rest and recuperation will increase also. For this reason a high intensity training cycle is recommended.

cycle	Level	Frequency	Workouts per week	Weeks on Cycle
one	Beginner	Every second Day	3	1
two	Intermediate	Every Third Day	2	1
three	Advanced	Every Fourth Day	2	2

Proper recuperation is required to maximize the gains from the conditioning program. The following are factors that can assist in recuperation:

1. High level of nutrition and supplementation throughout the day.
2. Minimum of 8-9 hours sleep each day.
3. Minimization of stress.
4. General health of internal organs.
5. Optimal hormone stimulation.
6. Adequate time interval between training sessions.

During the training cycles your strength and power should be increasing hence the requirement for longer rest periods.

CYCLE ONE

	Monday	Tuesday	Wednesday	Thursday	Friday	Saturday	Sunday
ek1	Workout1	Rest	Workout2	Rest	Workout3	Rest	Rest
ek2	Workout1	Rest	Workout2	Rest	Workout3	Rest	Rest

CYCLE TWO

	Monday	Tuesday	Wednesday	Thursday	Friday	Saturday	Sunday
ek1	Workout1	Rest	Rest	Workout2	Rest	Rest	Workout3
ek2	Workout1	Rest	Rest	Workout2	Rest	Rest	Workout3

CYCLE THREE

	Monday	Tuesday	Wednesday	Thursday	Friday	Saturday	Sunday
1	Workout1	Rest	Rest	Rest	Workout2	Rest	Rest
2	Rest	Workout3	Rest	Rest	Rest	Workout1	Rest
2	Rest	Rest	Workout2	Rest	Rest	Rest	Workout3

The above is a seven week cycle for explosive growth. The emphasis is on low reps, low sets and high intensity training with very heavy weights.

In between the seven week cycles you can take a week or two off for rest if required. Alternatively you can begin the next cycle immediately if your strength is increasing adequately.

You can also follow a sports training program or a volume and endurance cycle and use the above program for a power booster as required. Those of us in pursuit of strength and muscle growth can continue to cycle the above program until we have obtained the maximum possible benefit.

Volume Training

Volume training is the opposite of intensity training in that it requires a high number of sets and repetitions. Some muscle groups such as the calves, forearms and hands respond better to volume training. These muscle groups tend to consist of sinewy, short muscles.

Larger muscles use too much energy and take longer to recover with volume training.

Different cycles for muscle mass, endurance, strength, power etc are used to enable continued use of this principle over time and each is usually 1 – 3 months.

There is a popular gripper training program on the internet (the KTA program) that is largely based upon volume training. I strongly recommend this program as an aid to your Iron Palm training but be warned – its a tough regime and often results in injury.

Get a copy at:: www.cyberpump.com/ktaprogram/

I myself had carpel tunnel for a few weeks after doing the KTA but with massage and jow it soon went away. If you find this program is too intense they do have an introductory program also.

www.cyberpump.com/rrbt/

This is called the radical reps baseline program. If you are new to heavy duty grippers this is the one for you. Once again this is volume training.

Often it is argued that volume training in general is suited more to professional lifters who use steroids and there is some merit to this argument.

Progressive Resistance

What is Progressive Resistance?

Progressive resistance goes by many names such as progressive overload, muscular adaptation, increasing resistance etc. Basically in layman's terms it means that by increasing some aspect of stress on the muscle in each workout the body will respond by adapting to the stress. If the stress is too great the body will become over trained. Too little and the body will be under trained and growth may not occur.

This principle is the basic premise of resistance training and it's very important to design all of your routines around the progressive adaptation principle. In reality "progressive resistance" is a specific application of "progressive adaptation" as all aspects of physical fitness and development can be stimulated such as cardiovascular, flexibility and endurance (volume training). For the sake of this writing I will use the terms interchangeably although this is not strictly correct.

Some ways to Achieve Progressive Resistance...

The first thing to keep in mind is that gradual growth over a period of time leads to better results, so make sure that your increase in each training session is not too great. If you try and increase the stress on your muscles too fast, you will most likely end up with injuries that will keep you out of training. To achieve good progressive overload, you can try the following techniques:

1. For weight lifting, gradually increase the weight in each exercise. The best way to tell when to increase the weight is when you are able to achieve one or two more reps on the current plates that you are using. If you can do this, its time to lift a heavier weight.

2. You can increase the number of reps for any given exercise. If you

usually do 6, try and push it to 8, then to 10, until you feel your muscles getting really fatigued. This will develop muscular endurance.

3. Once you increase the reps, increase the sets. Add a set or two at the end of each exercise session – keep going until you reach maximum fatigue. You can also try super sets and giant sets.

4. Gradually reduce rests between sets – before your muscles completely relax, get started on the next set.

5. Train more frequently – allow your muscles enough time to recuperate and heal, but at the same time, try and increase the frequency of your training sessions. You will notice with time that your muscles recuperate much faster and you are able to train much more frequently.

6. It's a good idea to have a training partner or a spotter. Progressive resistance stretches you and your muscles to the maximum and you may need someone to give you that extra encouragement to keep going. And also to help you with the weights should you suddenly need to let go!

7. Increase the amount of time that your muscles are under tension. For example, if you are doing a dumbbell curl and you usually count to six, count to twelve. This means going for slower motions, but you will definitely feel your muscles respond to the stress with a greater burn and lactic acid build-up.

8. Increase the intensity by doing more "work" in the same period of time. This is not the same as decreasing rest periods or increasing poundage's but relates directly to the physics equation defining "work". In simple English it means using exercises that require the weight to be moved a greater distance EG: doing squats not leg press, full body pull ups not lat pull downs or dead lift not leg curls. Use full body exercises that involve a greater range of motion to move the weight not specialization or isolation movements.

So just how do the muscles adapt?

There are different forms as adaptation that can occur in muscle tissue as we have discussed. Most commonly weightlifters want greater muscle size, strength and endurance. When you train using adaptive levels of stimuli this causes a breakdown of tissue, which is replaced by new tissue. The body over compensates in response to the stimuli. If you are focusing on strength and power part of this will be to increase fast twitch fibre development and decrease slow twitch associated with endurance.

Muscular hypertrophy is a primary adaptation to increased resistance, as is increased capillary density in the muscles and increased strength of bone tissue. This process takes several weeks and is associated with increased protein synthesis. Hyperplasia can also occur and this is the splitting of muscle fibres to create new cells. Some research has shown that the ratio of fast to slow twitch fibres can be manipulated by adaptive conditioning.

How do you apply Adaptive Training to your routines?

Assess your training goals first. Do you want greater strength? larger muscles ? Once the primary objective has been established you can take some existing routines and plan them with progressive adaptation in mind. Progressive adaptation also lends itself to instinctive training so long as you are aware of your weights, sets and reps in prior workouts you can gently increase while avoiding being overly rigid in your schedule. Other people will prefer to plan everything with a training diary and achieve mini goals with each workout.

So the principle of progressive resistance is easy to understand and apply - but best of all it never fails.

NEGATIVE REPS

Negative reps emphasize the negative or eccentric part of an exercise. This normally means the lowering part of an exercise. Normally gravity is allowed to assist in lowering a weight but with negative reps we fight gravity with all out might. For grip training negative reps are also used on hand grippers but it is the tension of the spring rather than gravity that is resisted. Negative reps are very intense and break down muscle tissue to a great extent. For this reason you must factor in greater recovery periods if using them in your grip routines.

Forced Reps

Forced reps involve doing additional reps beyond failure. Normally this means some form of assistance is required. With hand grippers it means using your other hand to help. With weights it often involves having a training partner. Forced reps are a frequently used method of extending a set past the point of failure to induce greater gains in muscle mass and quality.

Periodization

Periodization involves a cycling of training to minimize burnout and fatigue. We briefly discussed this when talking about volume training. This cycling is broken down into mesocycles and macrocycles. A macrocycle is the overall plan and mesocycles are the mini cycles inside that time frame. Some of us may find this a very pedantic approach and prefer to follow a looser training schedule.

The proof comes in the form of results and many people are very successful with periodization. The problem is in determining which cycles to follow to achieve results.

The end goal of a macrocycle is to reach a peak goal in a year or so down the track. Generally this is broken down into preparatory, competitive and transitional phases with 80% of the time spent in preparation.

Mesocycles are generally 2-6 weeks in duration and various aspects of strength and muscular development can be cycled. In some sense periodization could be applied to non-strength qigong training. For example while doing your Iron Palm regime you could emphasize the flat bag work for some time, then the hanging bag etc but this would really be an issue of time management. In strength training it is an issue of physiological adaptation and recovery not time management. Your body can only withstand a period of intense training for a limited time.

Types Of Hand Strength

Pinch: This is used when the hand lifts an object isometrically and squeezes the fingers and thumb together to do so.

Crush: This is an exercise in which the hand can open and close under tension such as with hand grippers.

Extensor: This type of exercise applies force when the hand opens on the outside of the hand. Such as when one opens the hand in a bucket of steel shot.

Wrist Flexion: This is the familiar forearm exercise experienced with dumbbell and barbell wrist curls.

Open Hand: This is when the hand is not clenched and is supporting a great weight as you may experience while standing and holding a heavy bucket handle with the fingers.

Anatomy of the Hand

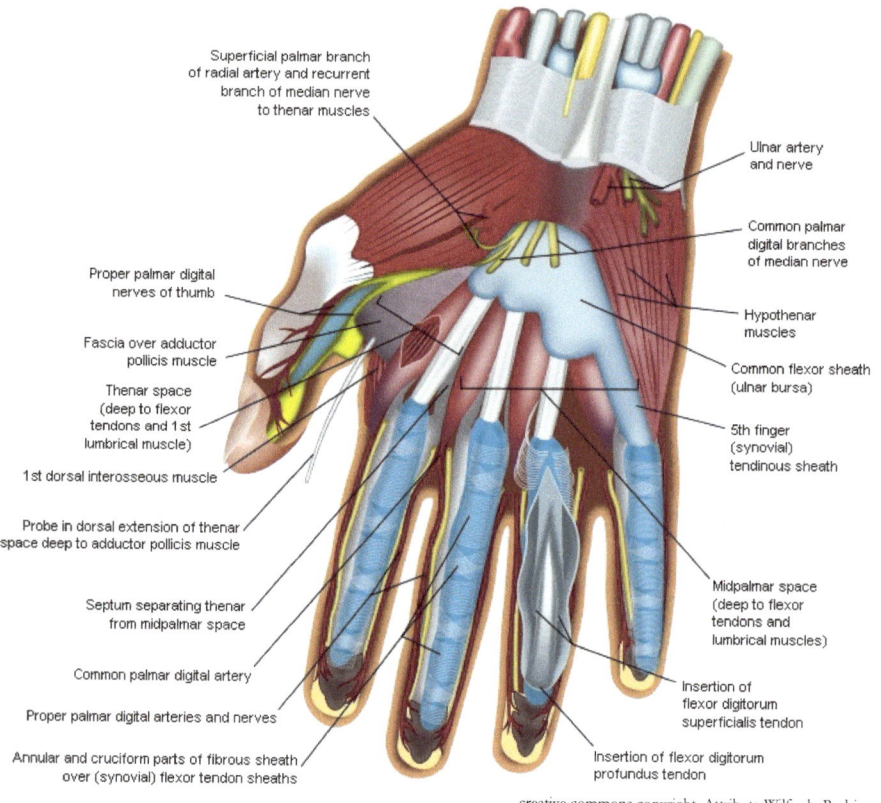

Nerves of the hand

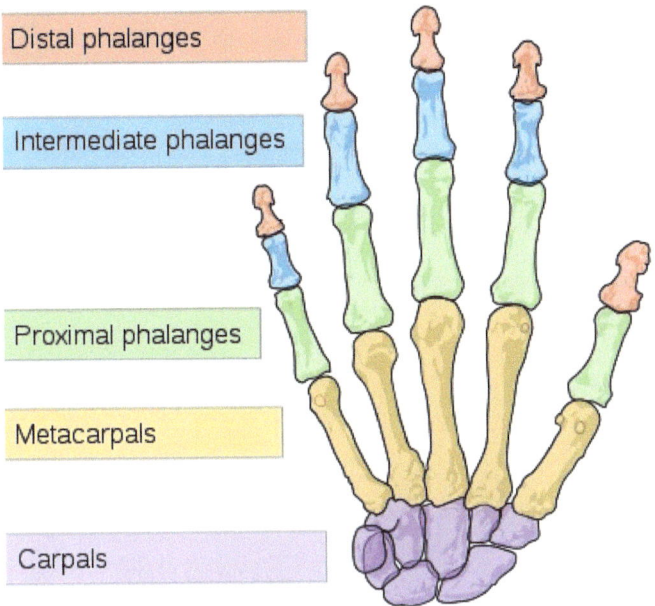

Bones of the hand

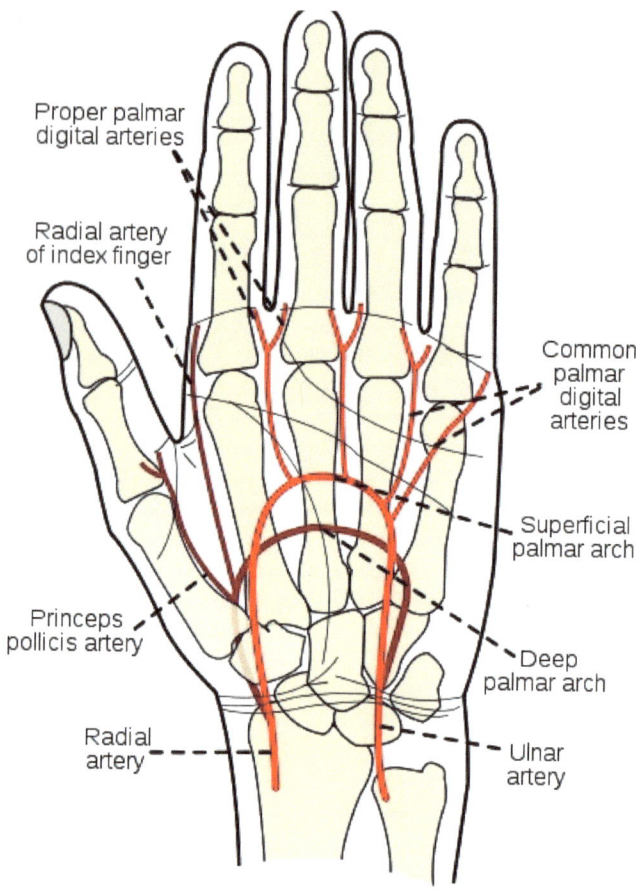

Blood Vessels of the Hand

Equipment

Hand Grippers

Heavy Grips

Heavy grips are an inexpensive option although the actual torsion will differ somewhat from the claimed value. It may be up to 30% more or less in some cases.

Values available are as follows: 100, 150, 200, 250, 300, 350 lbs.

Photo courtesy of www.heavygrips.com

Captains of Crush

These grippers are generally considered to be more accurate to the implied torsion and come in the following strengths: 100, 140, 195, 280, 365 lbs

As the strengths differ from heavy grips one can get a set of both and have a greater range of progression. This is important as if you aim too far ahead with your next gripper level it may cause a training plateau.

These grippers are available from www.IronMind.com who have a huge range of grip training gear and information.

John Brookfeild Grippers

John Brookfield is an unassuming looking guy but is actually known as "Mr Hands" and has the strongest grip in the world.

Photo courtesy of John Brookfield www.samsonscroll.com

John Brookfield's grip strength records:

- Tore 100 full packs of poker cards in half in 2 minutes 15 seconds.

- World Record Holder for bending 520 60-penny nails in 1 hour 42 minutes.

- World Record Holder for bending a 20 foot half inch dia (12mm) steel bar to fit into a small suitcase in 29 seconds.

John Brookfield's Endurance Feats:

John has achieved these feats of endurance without any specific preparation or training. At 47 years-old, many of John's weekly workouts are as difficult or often more difficult than these:

- 1200 kettle bell snatches in one hour with a 24kg kettle bell

- 302 kettle bell snatches with a 24kg kettle bell in the ten-minute snatch test

- 198 kettle bell snatches with a 32kg kettle bell in ten minutes

- Striking a 23kg hammer into a tyre for one hour non-stop (striking pace was 27 to 30 times per minute)

John has written two of the best books on grip and hand strength, which I highly recommend.

The Grip Masters Manual & Mastery of Hand Strength.

As well as breaking records and writing books John has come out with some of his own equipment.

The John Brookfeild grippers come with "screw in" handles that alter the leverage and thus give a range of resistance depending where you grip the handle. They are also long enough to squeeze with both hands.

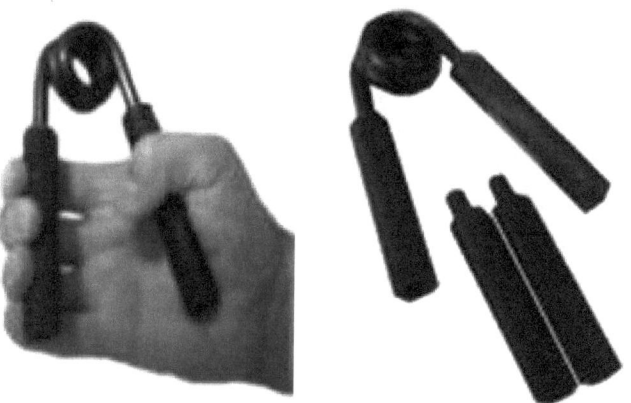

Photo courtesy of John Brookfield www.samsonscroll.com

Another great grip system is his battling ropes program. This involves using heavy tug of war style ropes in a whip like fashion. See his website for details.

Photo courtesy of John Brookfield www.samsonscroll.com

Beef Builder (Tetting Grippers)

Beef Builders come in 13 different levels of resistance.

110, 130, 165, 190, 235, 250, 300, 340, 365, 450, 535, 870, 1000

Now maybe with many months and years of very, very hard work you may reach 450 lbs – I hope so. I don't think anybody can close an 870 or 1000 lb gripper unless they are part gorilla but still its fun to try.

Beef builders take pride in the accuracy and quality of their product and are the main competitors with captains of crush. I have seen 400 & 500 lb grippers online also so have a snoop online if you want a full range of resistances and don't be shy to use multiple brands.

The place to discuss grippers online is www.GripBoard.com

Some of the greatest hand strength athletes in the world can be found talking grip training there. What you will find is that these guys are very pedantic about the resistance and go to the trouble of having their grippers lab tested so they know the exact value. Even then they are not happy as the torsion in the springs weakens over time.

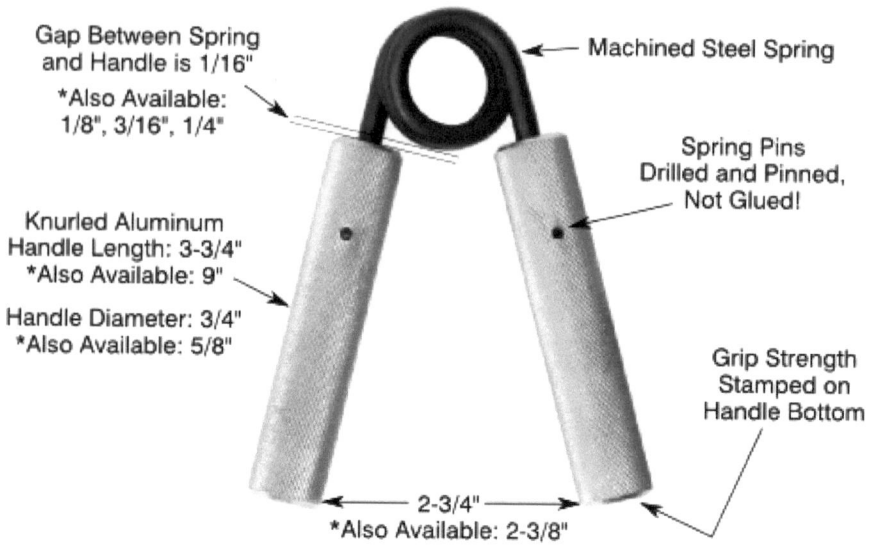

Photo courtesy of Weightlifters Warehouse

Beef Builders have a range of grip machines and gear you can find at the following URL:

www.wwfitness.com/gripstrength.html

Bone Crusher Grippers

The 400 & 500 lb grippers I mentioned are made by Bone Crushers. The full range is as follows:

100, 150, 200, 250, 300, 400 and 500 lbs

Iron Woody fitness is the distributor online www.ironwoodyfitness.com/hand-grips.php

Photo courtesy of www.ironwoodyfitness.com

Photo courtesy of www.ironwoodyfitness.com

Thumb Clamps (Spring Clamp)

This common and inexpensive hardware item is indispensable for thumb conditioning.

What a shame they don't come with pre measured resistances like grippers do.

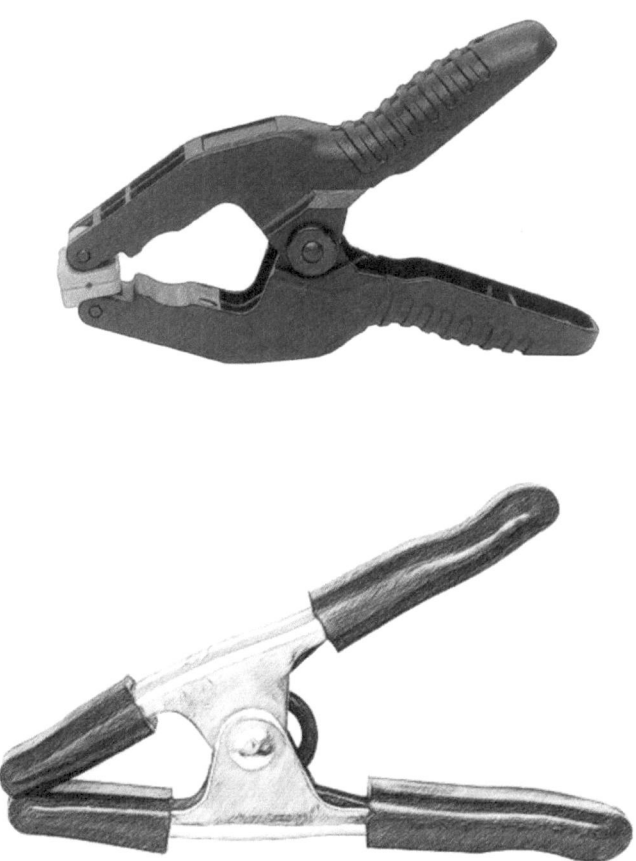

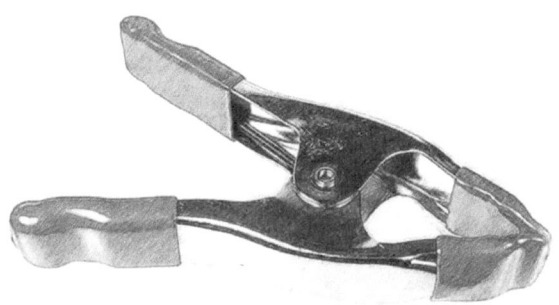

Buy several and start training with the easiest. Place your thumb on the top handle and squeeze for reps and sets just like gripper training.

Eagle Catcher

This is a classic piece of equipment familiar with many martial artists.

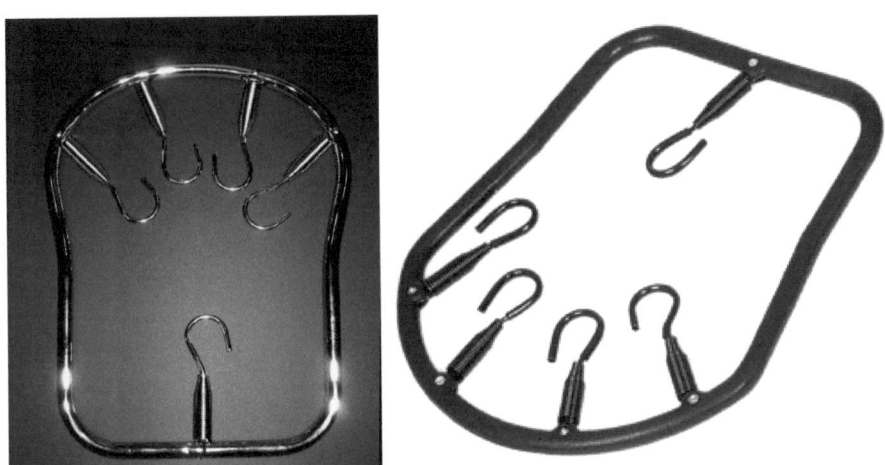

The eagle catcher is a must have along with hand grippers. Its great for finger strength. The only draw back is that the springs can't be upgraded to a higher resistance level. These days most come with a plastic frame so if you can get one that's metal do so.

Gripinator

The Gripinator is a specialized piece of equipment that uses weight plates along with grips similar to hand grippers. You may be lucky enough to find one of these on ebay. Priced between $300 & $400. You can make your own easily enough.

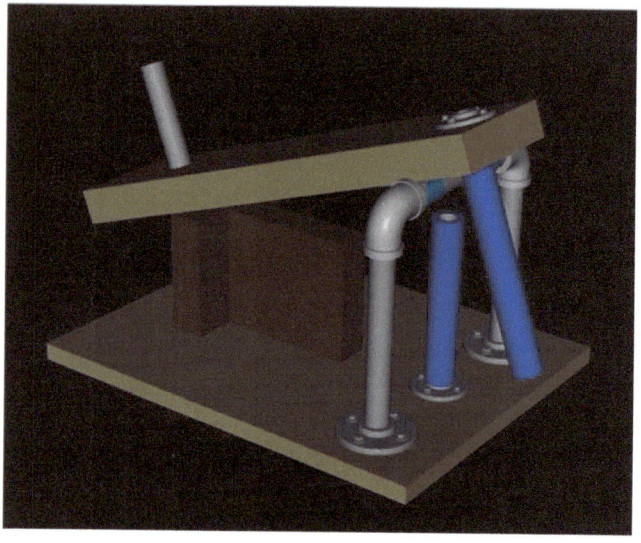

Photo courtesy of www.fractionalplates.com

Ivanko Gripper

The Ivanko Super Gripper is another Grip training classic. If you are serious you must get one. There are many sources for these online and they are not expensive. In fact one super gripper with an extra spring or two can provide far more resistance levels than all the single hand grippers combined. Plus it can reach tension levels that a human cannot achieve. The super gripper is used in exactly the same way as single grippers are so can be used to follow a program like KTA.

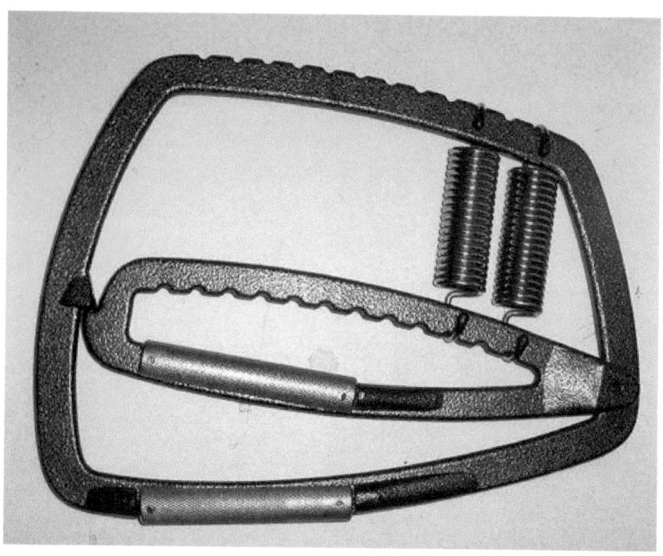

There is free software that provides the tension level for spring combinations and creates workout programs.

www.angelfire.com/ar/mathgod/sg/supergripper.html

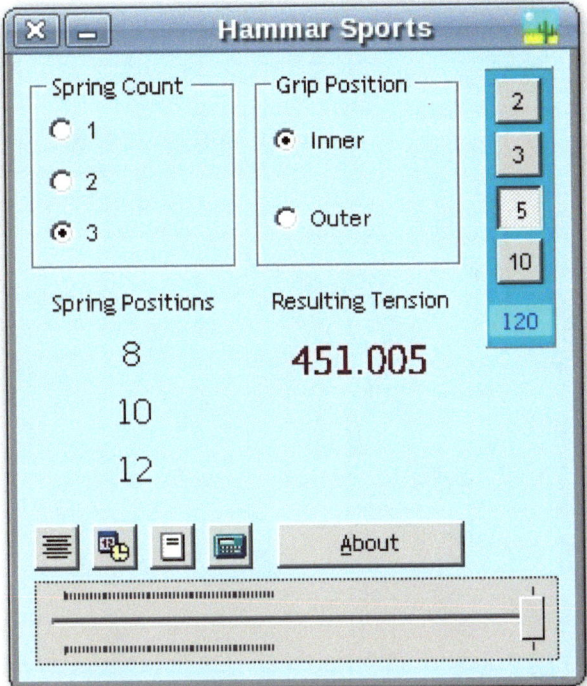

Iron Power Palm

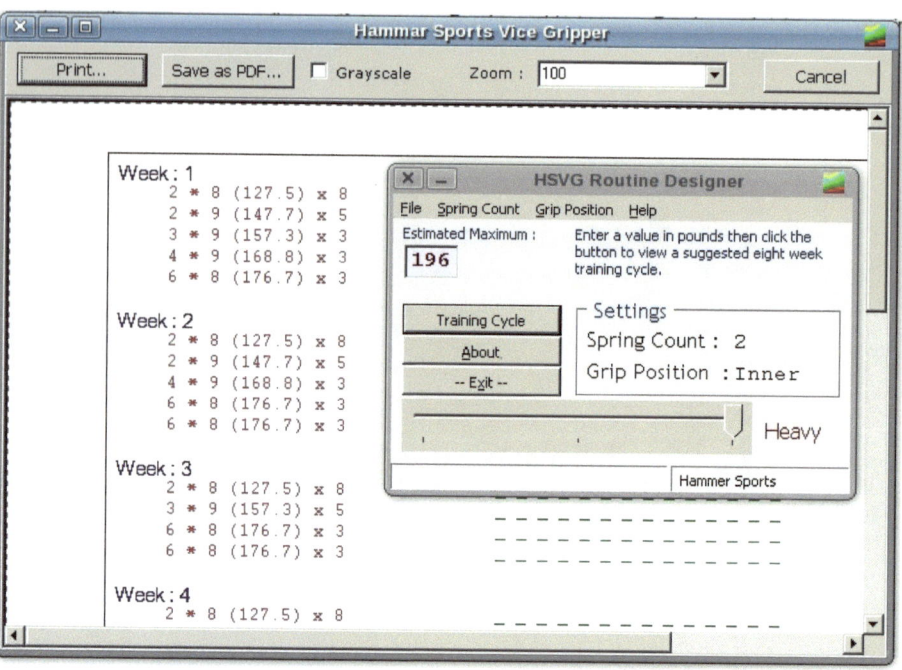

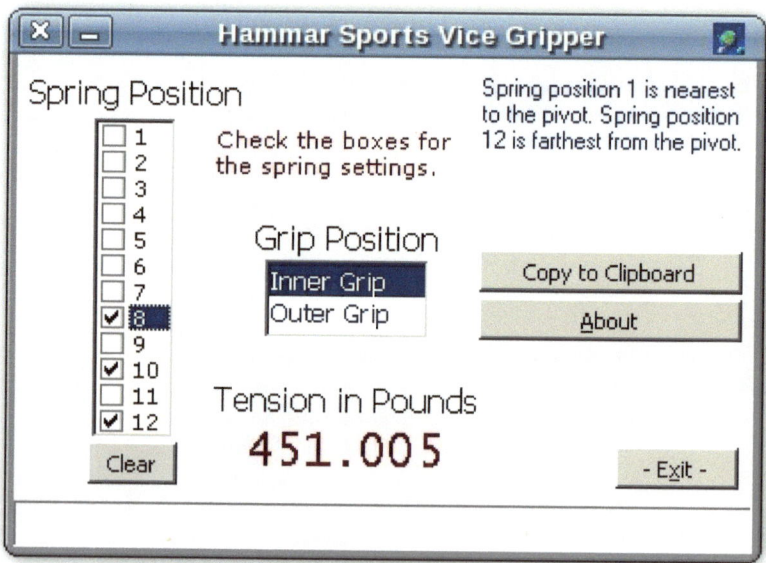

Wrist Roller

The Wrist Roller is a famous and easy to make piece of grip gear. To make your own you need a short bar such as a dumbbell bar and some thin rope. Or you can simply buy one.

There is a similar product called a grip stick that's used on the same way but has spring tension rather than a weight. Be careful with the gripstik as they tend to lock up. Really a Gripstik is only advantageous if you are on the move and don't want to haul heavy weight plates along. Otherwise just stick with a regular wrist roller as shown above. The hands can be parallel to the ground as shown above or if very heavy weight is used they can drop down.

Some people place the bar into a rack so all of the forearm and shoulder energy is put into rolling. This is a good idea. As you can see John Grimek had great forearm development.

Sledge Hammer

Sledge Hammer training places a great strain on the wrists. Basically you are fighting gravity and using leverage to do so. Hammers are used alone to flex the wrist in various directions (levering) or are used to beat heavy tractor or truck tires.

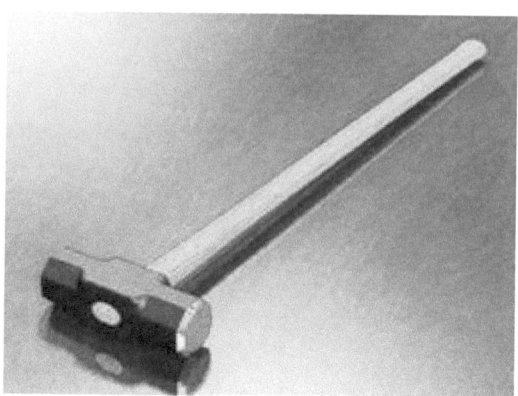

Manila Rope

Manila Rope is the thick heavy variety used in Tug-O-War. We mentioned the battling ropes program by John Brookfeild, which is a unique rope training program for grip & upper body strength. I suggest you get hold of Battling Ropes for more information on that. The other familiar way to develop grip with rope is climbing. This is a common test of upper body and grip power in the military.

Military rope climbers are encouraged to use the legs to twist around the rope as assistance but if you are climbing to develop grip you will want to avoid this.

Photo courtesy of United Staes Navy

Photo courtesy of United Staes Navy

Telegraph Tapper

These devices are used for developing thumb and finger strength much like spring clamps but have a different handle. No company has yet made a device with an ergonomic handle but at least with these devices you have variable resistance unlike the thumb clamps.

IronMind have one called Titans Telegraph.

IronMind Enterprises, Inc. I www.ironmind.com

As you see it's a simple leverage device that one could reproduce at home. An alternative is to buy screw on handles for your gripper set that enable the grippers to be pinched in the same way.

Elastic Bands

Elastic bands are used to train the extensor muscles of the hand that are neglected by all the squeezing and pinching exercises. IronMind has a range of elastic bands specifically for this purpose.

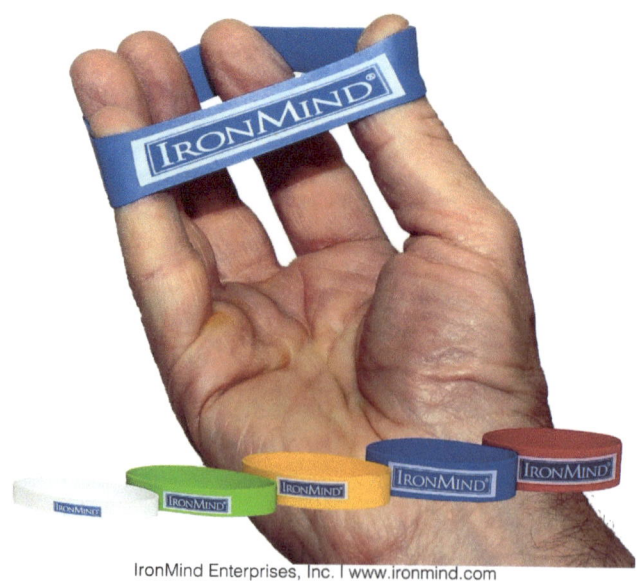

IronMind Enterprises, Inc. I www.ironmind.com

An alternative to this is to sink your hands into your Iron Palm jabbing shot bucket and open and close the hand to exhaustion against the pressure of the beans or shot. This will also exercise the extensor muscles. Extensor training is important as joint problems often occur as a result of imbalanced muscular development.

Thomas Inch Dumbell (Thick Bar Training)

Thomas Inch was a famous strongman of the past. One of his inventions is a wide gripped dumbbell that for most people is impossible to lift off the ground. The original Inch dumbbell was 172 pounds and 9 ounces.

To buy a replica Thomas Inch Dumbbell is actually very expensive. I have seen them advertised for $400. The good news if you really want one is that you can make your own from moulds.

The company to contact is www.SlatersHardware.com

Photo courtesy of www.slatershardware.com

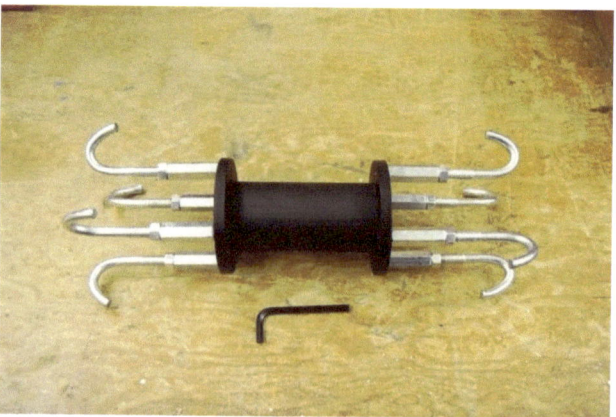

Photo courtesy of www.slatershardware.com

Slaters sell moulds for Atlas stones also. Various companies sell fat dumbbells and barbells these days. Another to look at is Fatgripz. These are rubber sleeves that you can simply slip on to your regular barbells and dumbbells. Best of all they are quite inexpensive.

Fat grip bars are much harder to lift and require great pinch strength in the hands and forearms. If you don't want to pay $40 for FatGripz you can cut a length of PVC or steel pipe to fit over your dumbbells. Alternatively you can make a sleeve from duct tape and newspaper. The end result is the same.

Photo courtesy of www.fatgripz.com

Pinch Grips (Block / Blob)

A number of different apparatus have been designed for Pinch Grip training.

The telegraph key already discussed is one, there also many block style handles to which weights can be attached. Popular block dumbbells are ideal pinch grip tools and instead of using the handle you lift vertically from one end of the dumbbell.

The "Blob" is a block weight made from one cut off end of a cast York dumbbell.

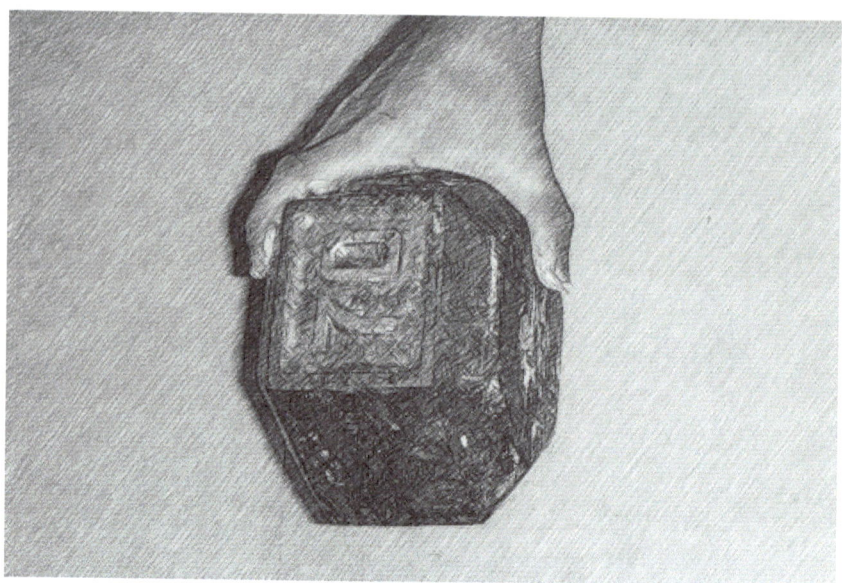

Gyroscope Balls

Gyro Balls use torque to produce resistance. Once you get the hang of using one you can adjust your speed to create more strain. These days many companies make these devices. Not a must have considering the vast selection of grip exercises but an interesting innovation.

Photo courtesy of www.dynaflex-intl.com

Photo courtesy of www.powerballs.com

Photo courtesy of www.powerxball.com

NSD and Dynaflex seem to be the main competitors and NSD claims to have a 13000 RPM device that has 80 lbs of torque. Personally I have found it difficult to learn how to use gyroscope balls.

Chinese Balls (Baodang Balls)

The final pieces of equipment we will discuss are Chinese Health Balls.

creative commons copyright, Attribute Manfred Werner

Now I cannot explain in a book how to use these. You must go to youtube and watch a few videos, then you will understand immediately. It is possible once you are skilled to use 4-5 balls in one hand. The exercises can also be performed upside down and with heavy large metal balls. Begin with just two balls at first.

GRIP EXERCISES

Hand Gripper

Introduction & Description:

Grippers are easy to come by in sports stores but most of these are of the light resistance variety. As strength trainers we require something a little more heavy duty. I recommend heavy duty grips which come in a variety of extra high resistances. Without heavy duty hand grippers or similar there are a couple of things you can do. One is to shorten the handles on regular grips. As the handle is a lever this makes the resistance much harder. Another is to attach two regular grips into one handle so it's twice as hard to squeeze. I have tried both of these and it worked OK. You can also purchase them in a variety of resistances right up to 350 lbs and more. I think you will agree a 300 lb grip is something to appreciate.

Anatomy & Biomechanics:

The normal squeeze method (with thumb up) works the whole hand but focuses on the bottom two fingers and the interior forearm. The inverted squeeze method occurs with the spring pointed down and focuses on the top two fingers and the top/outside of the forearm.

Step-By-Step Technique:

Grippers are grasped in palm of the hand and squeezed slowly and tightly. Naturally you will want to start with a lower resistance gripper such as 100 lbs. This is suitable as a warm up for experienced athletes or a beginning level for most females and new athletes. It really is an exercise that does not lend itself much to technique.

The normal squeeze is the basis for all gripper training. You are squeezing your hand and making a fist, then unsqueezing it. Do not bend the wrist but keep it locked. Set the gripper in your hand with the handle resting on your thumb pad, your little finger should barely wrap around the other handle. Now that the gripper is set, squeeze...HARD. The two ends of the gripper should touch each other.

It is possible to use isometric contraction when the fist is closed around the gripper and you can practice increasing the time you can maintain the contraction. This will result in a considerable lactic acid burn in the hand.

Dealing With Injury:

By keeping the wrist straight and gradually incrementing reps and resistance over time you should be able to avoid injury within this exercise. Chalk is a good idea to keep the grippers secured in your grasp. Lactic acid builds up quickly in the hands, especially with isometric grasping. A self-massage and application of eucalyptus or similar massage oil will have your hands feeling much better afterward (as the can become a bit sore). Unless the grippers slip from your grip while under tension, or if you do not have your wrist locked in a natural position you are most unlikely to experience an injury.

Variations:

The most novel idea I have come across as a variation on gripper training is to combine it with the hammer curl (which is a forearm exercise). By attaching a weight to the gripper so it hangs below you can perform a hammer curl and squeeze the gripper at the same time. Or you can simply squeeze the gripper and hold the weight isometrically in a hammer position. This is somewhat improvised, perhaps one day a clever person will design an apparatus specifically for this novel exercise.

Regular - The normal position with thumb pointed upward.

Inverted - The upside down position.

Isometric - We have discussed the isometric grip already. Basically the grip is locked at a stage in the squeeze. It does not have to be at the fully squeezed point to derive benefit.

Ball Squeeze - Get a tennis ball or similar and squeeze it in your fist for multiple sets and reps as you would grippers. This is actually a great warm up for gripper training and you are training the grip from a slightly different angle.

Alternative Grippers - There are the cheap low resistance plastic handled fitness grippers that you find in department stores, There are even an electronic variation of these out now but these are way too easy for serious strength training. Harbinger has an adjustable grip and there are martial arts grips that use a spring attached to each finger in a frame. I have found these devices to be very good for finger strength but painful as the rings dig into the fingers. Several companies make high quality high resistance grippers these days. You will have no trouble finding them online. There is also the "Extension Spring Gripper" or vice gripper which you can look up online.

Strap Holds: With the strap hold a strap holding a weight plate is gripped between the handles when you squeeze. This forces you to maintain pressure on the handles. There is also the secondary factor of the added weight being held which increases muscle tension.

Over crushes: The hardest part of closing a gripper is the final 1 cm. A way to train for this is the over crush. This involves filing part of the handle down so it goes beyond the normal range where the handles touch. Another trick is to place a washer around the top of the gripper so it only partially opens. This way you can train in the final 1-2 cm range.

Training Tips & Secrets:

Training the hands is like training any body part. To develop strength you must train with low repetitions and high resistance. The low resistance 100 lb grippers will be fine for warming up and for beginners but even if you can do 100 reps with these your actual hand strength will not develop much. Once you can do 20-30 reps with a certain resistance move up to something 50 lbs harder. You can also do descending sets with grippers of varying resistances. EG: 1 rep with 300 lbs, 3 reps with 250 lbs, 5 reps with 200 lbs and 10 reps with 150 lbs.

Oh yeah and if you want to know where to purchase these devices - Ebay has everything you want at a very low price.

Common Barbell & Dumbell Exercises

Pinch Grip

Introduction & Description:

The plate pinch is a purely isometric forearm exercise. It is also great in particular for thumb strengthening. Both flat and block weights can be used. Any heavy object can be used such as cinder blocks. Normal iron weights and thicker block weights are the most popular however any heavy item suitable for gripping with the fingertips is suitable.

Anatomy & Biomechanics:

The plate pinch is what is referred to as a "pad pinch" involving the thumb and fingers. This is not quite the same as a "lateral pinch" in which the thumb presses against the middle of the index finger. Strength in the "lateral pinch" will be greatly increased by plate pinching as the same muscles and ligaments are used. Pinching a plate activates the forearm muscles and hands. Pinching activates the flexor pollicus longus and the flexor digitorum profundus of the forearm.

The main muscles of the thumb include the abductor pollicis brevis, flexor pollicis brevis, pollicis longus, opponens pollicis and adductor pollicis. The term "thenar muscle" refers to the muscles of the thumb and "hypothenar" to those of the little finger. These two muscle groups act synergistically to squeeze the hand together.

Step-By-Step Technique:

Place either a single plate or two plates together and pinch between thumb and fingertips while standing. If using multiple plates put a short pipe through to connect them and prevent plate slippage. Hold the position until lactic acid build up is excessive. You can also try as a variation lifting the plate (held vertical between the legs) from the ground. This will add an element of difficulty. The plate can also be lifted up and down rather than just held in place. Sets and reps can be performed when lifting the plate. A static hold will result in isometric strength development.

Dealing With Injury:

The ligaments of thumb and fingers are placed under considerable strain doing plate pinches. Lifting gloves may afford some protection through padding but may also compromise the grip. Stretching is very relaxing and a must when performing strength conditioning. You may also wish to purchase some dexterity balls to stimulate circulation and nerve control.

Skin tearing and lesions are a very real possibility and duct tape or bandaging can be a good idea. Gloves are very effective at preventing lesions but compromise the pinch. You can experiment with fingerless gloves and tape.

Variations:

One or two hands - It seems a mute point as simply more weight can be used with two hands. It can be argued that you are less likely to drop the weight with a two-hand pinch. The two-hand pinch is more conductive to promoting muscle symmetry but greater intensity is possible with a single hand pinch.

Using multiple plates - Multiple plates allow for greater weight to be used and a wider grip which is more difficult. You need not be concerned about the plates slipping as all that you need do is pass a short dumbbell bar through the plates and collar them. Two 10 lb plates with a wide grip will be more difficult that a single 20 lb plate with a narrower grip.

Using other objects - Sand bags, jerry cans, rocks, cement blocks, block weights, anything heavy and gripable can be used in a pinch exercise so long as it can be clasped between thumb and fingers. You can also try an inverse method of pinch hanging from a bar or beam - not an easy exercise to perform.

Training Tips & Secrets:

Chalk is a must for plate pinch as it gives some friction to the grip. Also apply duct tape to prevent skin tears between the index finger and thumb. Train both for timed isometric hold and actual sets and reps of lifts. Isometrics tend to develop ligament and tendon strength while the sets and reps will develop the muscles of the hand and forearm.

Hammer Curl

Introduction & Description:

The Hammer Curl is a variation on the bicep curl that hits the Brachioradialis muscle thus making it a great exercise for developing the forearms. The biceps are still stimulated during the exercise but not to the extent of a regular bicep curl as now the Brachioradialis and Brachialis do some of the work also. Two heavy dumbbells are used but preferably not simultaneously. One arm is used for a rep and then the other. In this way more effort is concentrated on the arm doing the exercise. The Brachioradialis muscle is smaller that the bicep and so growth is apparent quite quickly from doing hammer curls. As a final remark - when it comes to the brachialis Hammer Curl is the number one exercise.

Anatomy & Biomechanics:

The primary muscle stimulated is the Brachioradialis (forearm) with the Biceps Brachii and Brachialis (below side of bicep) as secondary synergists. Stabilizer muscles include the Extensor Carpi Radialis, Flexor Carpi Radialis, Levator Scapulae, Trapezius and the Anterior Deltoid.

The hammer curl is similar to the bicep dumbbell curl except it targets the

Brachialis muscle on the side of the arm. If you place your other hand over this muscle while doing the exercise you can very clearly feel it swell as it contracts. It is not possible to do hammer curls with a barbell unless you have a roto-bar which has rotating grips welded into a barbell. The Brachialis plays a role in supination of the arm. In this exercise we do not supinate and pronate but keep the thumbs pointed skyward through the whole exercise.

Step-By-Step Technique:

With a dumbbell in each hand, stand with your arms hanging at your sides, and palms are facing each other. Keep your elbows locked into your sides. Your upper body and elbows should remain in the same place during the whole lift. And arm blaster or biceps bomber accessory is an ideal complement to this exercise.

Keep your palms facing each other, curl the weight in your right hand up in a semi-circle toward your right shoulder. Squeeze the biceps hard at the top of the lift and then slowly lower. Do not turn your wrists during this lift! You can also do one arm at a time and/or alternate.

Dealing With Injury:

Injury from the Hammer Curl is uncommon because the wrists are in a more natural position. Muscle tears are always a possibility of too much weight is used or if inadequate time has been allowed for recovery from previous conditioning. R.I.C.E is the acronym for rest, ice, compression & elevation. If you do experience a tear this is what you should do immediately. Bandage the arm and apply an ice bag to reduce swelling. Then go and see a sports physiotherapist for treatment.

Variations:

The Hammer Curl can be done with alternating arms or simultaneously. I prefer to do it alternating so I can focus my concentration but this does of course take twice as long to perform the exercise. One disadvantage of alternation is it is not as efficient if you use an arm blaster to lock the elbows. The arm blaster or bicep bomber is definitely recommended as MRI scans have proven that greater muscle stimulation occurs when using one - they definitely work. So it's not just a case of locking your arms to prevent cheating for safeties sake. More muscle adaptation will result as a consequence of using the device. As mentioned the Hammer Curl can also be done with a roto-bar, which is a great combination with the arm blaster. Variations to stimulate the forearm Brachioradialis include Barbell Reverse Curl, Barbell Reverse Preacher Curl, Cable Reverse Curl and Lever Reverse Preacher Curl.

Training Tips & Secrets:

I already gave you the best tip above - get a bicep bomber and a roto-bar. If you don't have this gear yet there is a work around.

What you can do is use a wall to prevent cheating. With a one arm exercise like Hammer Curl its best to bend the torso slightly and place the unused hand between the wall and just above the elbow of the arm doing the exertion. This prevents the elbow from rubbing against the wall and restricting motion.

Another tip is to do the exercise sitting down as in a seated concentration curl. Using the inner thigh to prevent the elbow cheating motion. This is a very comfortable way to perform Hammer Curls. In fact it feels more natural to do Hammer Curls in this way than bicep curls because of the positioning of the wrist. Apart from locking the elbow you must lock the wrist also. Its not difficult as the weight is not at the same angle as the wrist joint.

Just remember to perform the movement in a controlled manner without cheating.

Wrist Curl

Introduction & Description

The wrist curl is a great exercise to develop your forearms - in fact if you do it correctly and consistently, you are guaranteed to get great muscle into those as forearms as well as develop strength and increased flexibility. Its is also known as the supine wrist extension.

The wrist curl works on a specific pair of muscles – the extensor / flexor muscles, which run from your wrist to the elbow. It is the one that allows your forearm to literally flex up and down – without it, your forearm would not be able to move.

You can imagine therefore, the importance of building this muscle, particularly if you are bodybuilding. This muscle does a lot of hard work when you're lifting, so the more primed it is, the more ready you are for heavy lifting. The wrist curl exercise is a perfect for to build the flexor muscle.

Anatomy & Biomechanics

The wrist curl is a very specific exercise – it only stresses the wrist flexor & extensor muscles. In fact, it should not be done alone but should be done along with a combination of other exercises to make sure that all the muscles in your arm are getting the stress they need.

To do a wrist curl, you need to be seated with your forearms resting on your thighs. Make sure that your hands are completely free to move up and down, with palms facing up. You can do it using either dumbbells or a barbell. With fingers facing down, grab your dumbbells or barbell and lift it upwards and inwards. Raise and lower repeatedly, making sure that your knuckles face as high up as possible at the top of your raise.

Step-By-Step Technique

Sit on a flat bench and rest your forearms on your thighs. Make sure to have your feet firmly planted on the ground and your buttocks resting comfortably on the bench.

Lean forward so that your fingers are dangling over your knees and your palms are facing outwards.

Grasp you dumbbells or barbell. A normal grasp will do – you could try to have your thumbs go underneath the barbell or the weights, but some people find this uncomfortable.

Flexing your wrists, slowly curl up the barbell or dumbbells, bringing it towards your chest. As you move the weights up, exhale. Your forearms should remain on your thighs the entire time. Your knees act almost as a pivot for your wrists. You will feel the muscles in your forearms contract.

At the highest point, stop for a few seconds, tightening your muscles as you do so.

Inhaling, bring the weight back down to its original position. If you do this correctly, you will feel your forearm muscles stretch, but not completely relax. They should still remain a little contracted.

Repeat using your normal rep cycle, or as many times as you can.

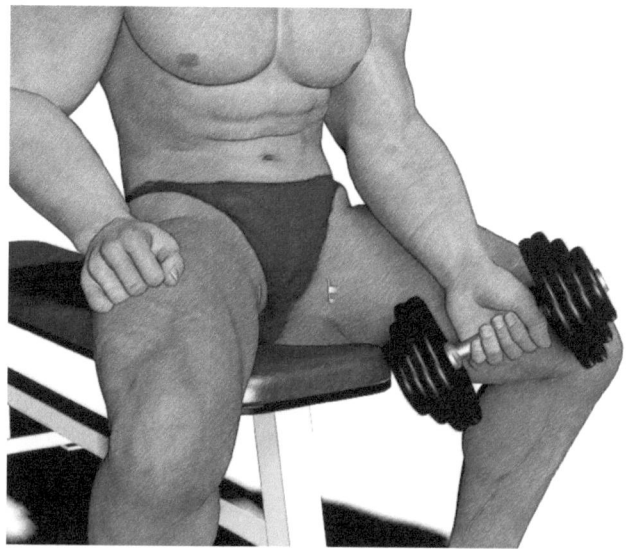

Dealing with Injury

You use your wrists and forearms for a lot of upper bodybuilding, so you must aim to keep them safe from injury. Wrists in themselves are quite delicate and need to be treated carefully. Before you start the exercise, make sure to warm up your arms by doing stretches. Follow instructions well to reduce risks.

Worse than tearing a ligament or tendon, you could actually sprain your wrist, which can be very painful and keep you from your workouts. Wrist injuries that are not attended can recur and can become quite bothersome in the future, so if you feel that your wrists are sore and painful, get medical advice. Take a break from training until your wrist feels better.

Variations

There are several different ways you can make your wrist curls more interesting:

1. You can do one arm first, using your other arm for support at the elbow. Do several reps on this one arm, and then switch and do the same for the other arm.

2. You can face your palms either down or up. Wrist curls with palms facing downwards (reverse wrist curl) work on the muscles on the outside of your forearms.
3. You can make variations on the speed at which you raise and lower the weights; you can try 2 or 3 different speeds within the same session. Control your speed though – if you do it too fast you may end up injuring yourself.

Training Tips & Secrets

Initially, you may it hard to maintain resistance. To help with this, try to keep your elbow at wrist height through out the motions.

If you can, dumbbells are preferable to a barbell. They allow you a greater range of motion and flexibility around the wrist.

Wrist curls work best after biceps or triceps training. It's a great way to wind down as you go towards completing an exercise session. It's also advisable because by this time, delicate wrist muscles will be warmed up and primed for stretching.

Keep building muscle and strength by increasing the weight that you lift, but this must be done gradually. A sudden increase in weight is one of the quickest ways to get a torn muscle or a sprained wrist.

This exercise moves around the joints in your wrist. For you to be successful, these joints must be well lubricated. Look into your diet for foods that increase lubrication between joints. This is useful for your whole bodybuilding regime as well.

Preacher Wrist Curl

Introduction & Description

We are still working on toning up those forearms and building some muscle into them, as well as strengthening your wrists. It's time to try the preacher wrist curl. Like the name suggests, you will need to use a preacher bench for this one. This exercise aims particularly at your wrists and your forearms. In fact, if you have already been through a wrist curl exercise, this one should come easy, because the only difference is that you are sitting on a preacher bench.

Anatomy & Biomechanics

This is a pretty specific exercise and it aims at building your inner forearms, specifically the wrist flexor muscles and the brachioradialis in the forearms. Preacher wrist curls are pretty much an isolated exercise – you will be using a very specific part of you body to lift the weight. The usual preacher curls that you have probably done aim at building your upper forearms, but because we are raising the weights only to wrist level here, you will now be stressing the lower forearms. As you do this, you will also be stressing your wrist flexors.

You can try the exercise using either a barbell or dumbbells, but because you are sitting on a preacher bench, a barbell would be more stable.

Step By Step Technique

Sit yourself at the preacher bench with your chest against the bench. Your armpits should be in contact with the bench. Make sure that your feet are firmly positioned on the ground and that your arms are comfortably rested on the bench pad.

Extend your arms over the preacher bench pad and keep them straight. This is an exercise that will use your wrists and forearms, so make sure you position them comfortably enough to deal with all the lifting.

Grasp your barbell or your dumbbells, palms facing upwards. A good way to do this is to use a spotter, so that they can hand you the barbell or dumbbells once you are seated on the bench. If you don't have a spotter, your bench will probably have a bar where you can rest your barbell or dumbbell to reach it easily.

Flexing your wrists, slowly curl up the barbell or dumbbells, bringing it towards the preacher bench and thus towards your chest. As you move the weights up, exhale. Your forearms should remain on the preacher bench the whole time. The bench acts almost as a pivot for your elbows, allowing your wrists to move upwards and downwards. You will feel the muscles in your forearms contract.

At the highest point, when your knuckles are facing upwards, stop for a few seconds, tightening your forearm muscles as you do so.

Inhaling, bring the weight back down to its original position. If you do this correctly, you will feel your forearm muscles stretch, but not completely relax. They should still remain a little contracted.

Exhale and repeat the motion as many times as you usually do in your exercise routine, or simply until you feel you can't go on any more.

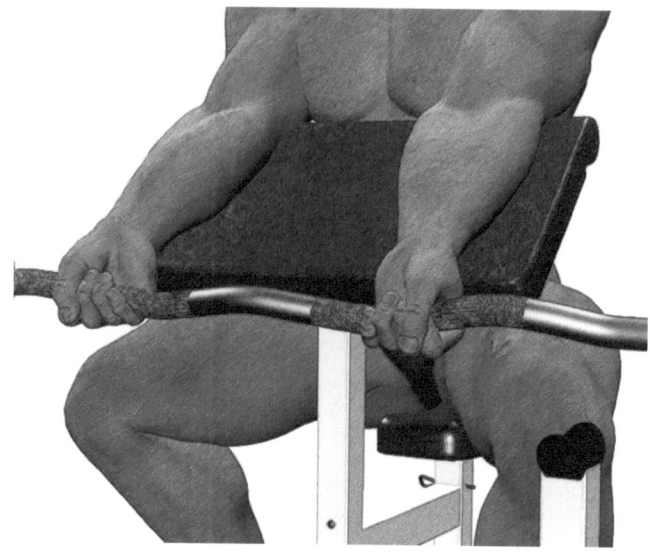

Dealing with Injury

You are using your forearms and wrists for this exercise, and you need to be careful not to hurt either. Injuries are likely to occur to the wrist flexor and the brachioradialis in the forearms. It's very important that as you curl your wrists, you make sure that your forearms are well rested on the preacher bench – this eliminates chances of injury.

As with any other exercise, start by warming up your body with stretches. To make sure that your muscles are even more primed, this is an exercise that you can do after you have done your other upper arm exercises. Make sure to follow instructions.

If you feel any strain or irritation in your forearms or wrists, take a break. Preacher wrist curls can also hurt your elbow joint because it's used as a pivot. Make sure that as you lower the weight back to its original position, you do not do it too fast and "yank" your elbows downwards.

Variations

To make your preacher wrist curls more interesting, you can:

If you are using dumbbells, start with one arm and do as many reps as you can use this arm before you switch to your other arm.

Reverse the direction of your palms as you grasp the weights. Initially, your palms were facing upwards towards you. Now grasp with your palms facing downwards towards the floor and curl your wrists upwards until your knuckles are facing downwards.

You can use an exercise ball as your preacher bench if you don't have one or even just for variation. You need to be careful with this though, it's easier to get an injury on your forearms, wrists or elbow with an exercise ball than with a preacher bench. It's also recommended that if you use an exercise ball, do one arm at a time.

Try to do this exercise while sitting and then while standing. This will place different amounts of stress on the different muscles that you are trying to exercise.

Training Tips & Secrets

Your wrists are delicate and your wrist flexor muscles are rarely worked. Start with a smaller weight, and gradually increase to reduce the risk of injury.

Before you do the preacher wrist curl, warm up with other upper body exercises. By the time you get to lift weights with your wrists, they will be pretty primed and ready. Preacher curls are recommended.

You will probably feel quite some strain when you try this exercise the first time. The best thing to do is approach it gradually, for short periods of time and as mentioned earlier, light weights.

Reverse Barbell preacher Curl

Introduction & Description

Its all in the name – reverse barbell preacher curl: you are going to be doing a barbell curl on a preacher bench, but in reverse so that your grip is facing downwards towards the floor and not upwards. It's a great exercise to build both upper and lower forearms, and with consistency you'll soon have a nice pair of biceps to show for your efforts!

Anatomy & Biomechanics

The reverse barbell preacher curl works mainly on the brachialis, brachioradialis and pronator teres, filling your biceps with muscle, as your forearms also benefit from all the lifting. It's an isolation exercise that uses a small group of muscles, and has very limited movement. What makes it even more limited is the fact that you're sitting on a preacher bench with your arms completely rested on the pad, so that there is very limited motion to the rest of your body. This results in maximum stress being put on the bicep muscles and this means you can achieve results very quickly if you do it correctly and consistently.

The technique is quite simple – you sit at the preacher bench, extend your arms over the pad and grab your barbell. As you lift and lower the weights, you feel your bicep muscles tighten and relax, but you will notice that all the strain goes to the biceps and a little to the forearms.

Step-By-Step Technique

Sit yourself at the preacher bench with your chest against the bench. Your armpits should be in contact with the bench. Make sure that your feet are firmly positioned on the ground and that your arms are comfortably rested on the bench pad.

Extend your arms over the pad and keep them straight. This is an exercise that will use your biceps and forearms, so make sure you position them comfortably enough to deal with all the lifting.

Grasp your barbell, palms facing downwards towards the floor. Use a normal grip – your thumbs do not have to go around the bar.

Slowly lift the weights towards your chest – your arms must remain in the same position on the bench at all times and other parts of your body should not be in motion. Your wrists will curl inwards as you lift, with your knuckles eventually facing your chest.

Keep lifting the weight until your forearms are vertical to the floor – at this point, the weight will be pretty close to your chest. At the height of the lift, pause for a second and tighten your biceps.

Lower the weights slowly until your arms are fully extended over the pad once again. As you get to full extension of your arms, you will feel your bicep muscles relax.

Exhale and repeat the motion as many times as you usually do in your exercise routine, or simply until you feel you can't go on any more.

Dealing with Injury

Like with the normal preacher curl, the commonest injuries are to the elbows and to the specific muscles in the biceps – the brachialis, brachioradialis and pronator teres. As you bring the weights down, you may over-extend your arm and overstrain your elbows. This can lead to biceps tendonitis or anterior capsule strain. These are just complex names for muscle abrasions or tears in the biceps. Remember the muscles involved in this exercise are pretty small and this makes them susceptible to injury if not handled carefully.

It's also pretty easy to bruise or even sprain your wrists as you are now using them in reverse. Be careful to start with a small weight and gradually add to this to avoid this.

As with any exercise routine, make sure that you follow instructions. Also, this exercise requires specific equipment, so try to avoid improvising on a bench as you may not get the padding just right and may end up injuring your arms or elbows.

If you hurt yourself, take a break from exercising that particular set of muscles for some time. Of course, if you feel it's serious, seek medical advice.

The good thing is, though, that biceps heal pretty quickly, although on the other hand, an injured wrist may take quite a while to heal.

Variations

There are several variations that you can try to make your reverse barbell preacher curls:

You can do them either sitting down or standing up. If done standing up, you need a different model of a preacher's bench than if you do it sitting down. If you can access both in your gym, all the better. Do a session while sitting down, and then vary it by doing another standing up.

Instead of using a barbell, you can use dumbbells. You can start the exercise with one arm, and then alternate. Both arms should rest on the bench although only one is doing the lifting. Keep switching but make sure that the reps are equal on each arm so that you get a balanced stretch on both sides.

You can do this exercise while relaxing at home too. Use an exercise ball as your bench. Extend your arm over it, and then grab the weight and lift and lower. Careful though - with this one, because of the curve of the ball, you can over-extend your elbow and end up with injuries!

You can use a reverse grip. The initial time you tried it, your palms were facing downwards. Now try grasping your weights with your palms facing upwards, as in a normal barbell preacher curl.

Training Tips & Secrets

To make your reverse barbell preacher curls more successful you can try the following:

Whether you are sitting or standing, make sure that throughout, your back remains straight. Your biceps and forearms will end up doing all the lifting and getting that much stronger.

Put a thrust into your initial lift, but make sure to lower the weight slowly to avoid over-extending of your elbows.

Keep building muscle and strength by increasing the weight that you lift, but this must be done gradually. A sudden increase in weight is one of the quickest ways to get a torn muscle or a sprained wrist. In fact, just like a normal preacher curl, it is recommended that you start with a small weight as you are dealing with muscles that are pretty small.

Your elbows will move around quite a bit during this exercise - keep your joints well lubricated by eating the right food.

Reverse Wrist Curl

Introduction & Description

Also known as the pronated wrist extension this is very much like a regular wrist curl (supine wrist extension), but as the title suggests, in this one your palms face downwards instead of up. You can either use a barbell or dumbbells. You can do it either sitting or standing but the seated position is favorable in terms of muscle isolation. It strengthens the upper biceps and outer forearms. The targeted muscles are relatively quite small, and therefore not very strong, and you may just want to start with very light dumbbells or just a barbell without plates if you are a female or beginner.

Anatomy & Biomechanics

This exercise mainly works on the wrist extensors to strengthen the opposing sides of the forearms. If you do it well, and consistently, you should notice your forearms get bigger and firmer, and your grip will generally get stronger. As earlier mentioned, the palms face the opposite position as in the wrist curl, and Reverse Wrist Curl are therefore targeted at a very particular set of muscles in the forearm (wrist extensors). The reverse wrist curl should therefore be done together with other arm exercises to get maximum strengthening of the full forearm, which in turn strengthens the elbow joint. No stabilizer muscles are predominant in the seated version of this exercise and the arm is fully supported by the bench or thighs.

Doing the standing variation the biceps is contracted isometrically. There is also an isometric exertion on the brachioradialis of the forearm. Some prefer to do the standing version to combine the brachioradialis and wrist extensor stimulation.

Step-By-Step Technique

Sitting:

Sit on a flat bench and rest your forearms on your thighs. Make sure to have your feet firmly planted on the ground and your buttocks resting comfortably on the bench.
Lean forward and with your arms still on your thighs, and your palms facing the floor or downwards.
Grasp you dumbbells or barbell. A normal grasp will do.

Flexing your wrists, slowly curl barbell or dumbbells or upwards, bringing it towards your chest but without getting your arms off your thighs. As you move the weights up, exhale. Your knees act almost as a pivot as your wrists move up and down. You will feel the muscles in your fore-arms contract.

When your knuckles are at their highest point, stop for a few seconds, tightening your muscles as you do so.

Inhale and bring the weight back down to its original position. If you do this correctly, you will feel your forearm muscles stretch, but not completely relax. They should still remain a little contracted.

Repeat using your normal rep cycle, or as many times as you can.

Standing:

Stand upright with your feet firmly planted on the floor. They should be about a foot apart. Make sure that you are stable.

Grasp the dumbbells or barbell with your palms facing the floor.

Start to lift the weights, keeping your arms straight and your elbows next to your chest.

As you lift the weight towards your chest, your elbows will fold so that eventually, your forearms will be vertical to the floor. Feel your muscles tighten. When the weight is at your chest, hold it there for a second, contract your muscles and then lower it again slowly to its original position.

Dealing with Injury

Just as with the wrist curl, caution should be taken with this exercise. Since you use you wrist and forearms a lot in your upper bodybuilding, you want to have these muscles and joints always at their best.

Make sure to warm up before an exercise. Since the muscles that are being worked are small, you need to take extra caution not to sprain them during the exercise.

In particular, be wary of a wrist injury – it can keep recurring and become quite bothersome. If you sprain your wrist, it's always best to seek medical advice. Otherwise, for muscular injuries, it is advisable that you take a break from training the injured muscle until pain subsides.

As a great deal of stress is placed upon the wrist joints in this exercise as it is in all forearm training its important to take care of your joints. Stretching is always a good idea for the hands, fingers and wrists prior to exercise with weights. Special liniments can be applied to the hands and wrists after training to aid recovery. Also a great nutritional supplement to support joint function is omega 3 oil & glucosamine, which will help to maintain well lubricated and properly functioning joints.

Variations

The main variation with this exercise is that you can either sit or stand, or for maximum benefit, use both techniques in a session. Other things you can try are:

You can do one arm first, using your other arm for support at the elbow. Do several reps on this one arm and then switch and do the same for the other arm.

You can make variations on the speed at which you raise and lower the weights; you can try 2 or 3 different speeds within the same session. Control your speed though – if you do it too fast you may end up injuring yourself.

Try the preacher reverse wrist curl. This is done on a bench that supports the upper arms thus preventing cheating.

Cables, barbell or dumbbells can be used to provide resistance.

Training Tips & Secrets

You will notice that the tips here are very similar to the tips in the wrist curl. This is because you are exercising a similar group of muscles and they should more or less be treated in the same way. You could try the following:

Use dumbbells, they are preferable to a barbell. They allow you a greater range of motion and flexibility around the wrist.

Reverse wrist curls work best after a biceps or triceps training. Use them to wind down as you go towards completing an exercise session. It's also advisable because by this time, delicate wrist muscles will be warmed up and primed for stretching.

Keep building muscle and strength by increasing the weight that you lift, but this must be done gradually. A sudden increase in weight is one of the quickest ways to get a torn muscle or a sprained wrist.

Try doing the exercise with an arm blaster or easy curl bar to limit movement of the elbows in the standing variation.

This exercise moves around the joints in your wrist. For you to be successful, these joints must be well functioning well. Look into your diet try foods that improve function of joints such as omega3 oil & glucosamine. This is useful for your whole bodybuilding regime as well.

Try different support of the arm, preacher bench, try kneeling and using a regular bench.

Zottman Curl

Introduction & Description

Let's now put some muscle on those forearms and biceps. The most effective exercise you can possibly do, with quick results, is the Zottman curl. The Zottman curl is named after old timer and famed body builder, George Zottman. Typically, it is an exercise that is meant to quickly beef up your forearms and your biceps. It mainly targets the brachioradialis, which is the muscle that runs down the thumb side of your forearm. It's the muscle of the forearm that acts to flex the forearm at the elbow, and so runs all the way from your forearm to your bicep.

If you are bodybuilding or weight training, this is a muscle you must target because the more you strengthen it, the more you become much more flexible in your other lifting. Even if you do not have biceps, or beefy forearms to start with, give the Zottman curl a try and soon, you will notice an impressive change. In fact, any arm workout program cannot be complete without this exercise, as it introduces balance between the upper and lower arm muscles.

Anatomy & Biomechanics

This exercise is actually quite straight forward, but it's great because it is so rewarding, and it does not take very long to see results. You lift a pair of dumbbells as you would if you were doing a normal curl. When the dumbbells get to your chest, you turn your palms so that they are facing outwards from your chest. The dumbbells are now at your chest level – lower them slowly with your palms still facing outwards. As you make this upward and downward motion, you will feel the muscle in your inner forearm stretch. Repeat using your normal rep cycle, or as many times as you can.

An additional benefit with this exercise is that as you twist your wrists at the top of the curl, you get to stretch additional muscle that you otherwise would not in a regular dumbbell curl.

Step-By-Step Technique

Grab your dumbbells by your sides with your thighs slightly bent. Your palms should face forward just as they would with a regular curl.

Keep your elbows at your sides and slowly curl both the dumbbells upwards. As the dumbbells reach your shoulder level, squeeze your bicep muscles as hard as you can.

Then make a clockwise circular motion so that eventually, your palms are facing inwards (in a normal curl, like a dumbbell curl, you would raise the dumbbells up and down, but with this one, you will need to rotate).

Lower the dumbbells slowly – with the rotation in the previous step, your palms will now be facing the floor.

Lower your arms back to your starting position, and once there, turn your palms forward again. That completes a cycle or a rep.

Repeat using your usual number of reps, or as many times as you can, but take a minute's break between reps.

If you are doing it correctly, you will feel your muscles tighten as your dumbbells get to chest level, and relax as your lower the weights back to your knee level.

Dealing with Injury

As with any other exercise, the key to avoiding injury is making sure that you follow instructions properly. Before you start your exercise, prime your muscle through a warm up – this also stimulates and readies the central nervous system for maximum stimulation.

Typical injuries that can arise from this exercise are torn muscles and ligaments, or sprained wrists from the rotation of the dumbbells. Be careful about this, as an arm injury will obviously put you out of arm training for a while.

Should you get an injury, and depending on how serious it is, you should give your arms a break to allow the torn muscle or ligament to heal. If it's more serious, you should of course see a doctor.

It is also possible to get the muscles around your wrists irritated and torn if you do not straighten them at the top of your curl before you rotate. This can be quite serious – if it happens, have a doctor take a look at your wrists.

Variations

<u>Alternate the lifts:</u> Start by lifting the left dumbbell only in the way we have described, and then alternate to your right. Do this a few times, and then do it simultaneously – as you lower the left, you raise the right.

<u>Sit at a bench or stand:</u> You can either sit or stand to do a Zottman curl. It's best to use both, so that different muscle groups come into play with each alternate shift. Have a session while standing, and another session while sitting.

<u>Reverse the curl:</u> Your initial curl was with palms facing outwards and ended in them facing the floor. Now reverse this – start with your palms facing the floor and end with them facing inwards. Be careful with this one though, this reversal can easily give you an injury if you are not quite ready for it.

Training Tips & Secrets

Here are a few tips to make your Zottman curls more comfortable and to help you see faster results:

Always increase the weight of your dumbbells gradually. The key to growing any muscle successfully is to grow it gradually, so start with a light weight, and gradually add as you build your strength.

As you lift and lower your dumbbells, keep your upper arms still. This minimizes risk of injuries and ensures that you are stressing the correct muscles.

If you have not done curls before, it is recommended that you start with simpler curls like barbell curls and then eventually move to Zottman curls. These simpler curls will prime your muscles for this more intense curl.

Reverse Barbell Curl

Introduction & Description:

The reverse barbell curl is a very popular forearm exercise. It is a simple exercise to perform and essentially the same as regular curls in execution except that the position of the palms is reversed. For this reason reverse barbell curl is not a primary exercise for the biceps and it also does not totally isolate the forearms. Both the forearm and bicep are stimulated. You will definitely feel the most force in your forearms.

Anatomy & Biomechanics:

The brachioradialis of the forearm is the main muscle exercised with the reverse curl. It is the main elbow flexor muscle. It also plays a part in pronation and supination. It is clearly visible running along the top part of the forearm. The biceps brachii is a secondary muscle used in the reverse barbell curl. It is also a synergist as is the brachialis. Stabilizer muscles include the anterior deltoids, trapezius, Levator Scapulae and wrist extensors. The bicep is only of secondary importance in this exercise.

Step By Step Technique:

Essentially the exercise is performed similarly to the barbell biceps curl except that the palms are now reversed and facing downward. This places the pressure on the forearm rather than the bicep. It is referred to as an overhand grip and focuses on the outer forearm muscles in particular. Start with the arms shoulder width apart and the barbell resting against the thighs. Raise the barbell until it is above the upper chest then lower back to the original position. It is important not to cheat by using momentum. So avoid excessive knee bending and swinging of the torso. As with the bicep curl an arm blaster device can be used to stabilize the elbows. A more explosive motion can be used on the upward phase if you so choose but lowering (negative) should be smooth and controlled.

The biceps can be squeezed at the top of the exercise motion and reps should vary between six to twelve. Because of stress on wrist and elbow joints this exercise is best not performed purely for power with super heavy weight. Generally less weight is used in the reverse barbell curl that the bicep curl.

Dealing With Injury:

The wrists are quite vulnerable in this exercise particularly if you have small wrists. Be sure to keep them locked throughout the entire motion to avoid sprain or a ligament tear. While using a normal barbell the angle of the wrist is somewhat unnatural so an EZ-curl bar is preferred. Another precaution is to avoid over adaptation by using too much weight on the bar. Micro blood vessel bursts are also common in the forearms for some people as this body part is quite vascular. What it looks like is a small round lump under the skin. This is harmless and usually goes away after some weeks or months but if agitated can develop into a varicose vein.

The elbow joint is also placed under considerable strain during reverse curls. Be sure to lock the elbows and use an arm blaster device if you are able to get one from Amazon or ebay.

Variations:

The EZ-curl bar is considered by many to be a "must" for this exercise as it allows a more natural positioning of the wrists. Likewise as already mentioned an "arm blaster" or "bicep bomber" is also a must have. Dumbbells are a popular alternative to the barbell. There is no reason why you cannot perform the exercise with kettle bells, a chest expander or cables either. The barbell has the advantage of providing for symmetric force on both forearms at once. Rope curls are done using the weight stack at the gym. They also stimulate the brachioradialis as do Zottman curls which can be performed at home with dumbbells.

Training Tips & Secrets:

Keeps your wrists locked throughout the exercise. This will ensure maximum concentration on the brachioradialis. Likewise the elbows should remain locked and close to the sides of the body. Keep your attention on form during the exercise especially with the elbows as it is easy to let them move out to the sides while performing the reverse barbell curl. While an explosive can be use on the positive part of the exercise this is not a requirement and a slow controlled raising of the barbell should be practised in some workouts also.

As for your grip you can experiment with gloves or chalk powder. The hand is pointed downward so handgrip if weak can present a limitation in this exercise.

Wrist Roller

Introduction & Description

Its time for to work on those forearms again, but how about an exercise that stresses a little more than just forearms? The wrist roller targets several muscles at once. It's actually considered to be one of the best forearms exercises that you can do. Great body builders say that the results are great, and that if you are consistent, you will have great looking forearms in a very short time. What makes it even better is that you do not have to buy expensive equipment – you can fashion your own wrist roller right at home.

The range on motion involved in a wrist roller, together with the flexibility ensure that you get a complete forearm and wrist exercise at once. Your shoulders also end up getting a part of the action, and it's this combination of stressed muscles that makes it so great.

Anatomy & Biomechanics

In a wrist roller, we are targeting the forearm flexors, the Brachioradialis, and to some extent the wrist flexors. The wrist flexors are mainly exercised by the backwards and forwards motion of both the forearms and the wrists during the exercise, while the forearms are strengthened by the weight of the wrist roller itself.

As a matter of fact, baseball players use this exercise often because of the range of exercise it provides to the different muscles. It improves their pitching ability and gives them powerful throws.

To do this exercise, you need to have a wrist roller directly in front of you, resting in your grip with your arms parallel to the floor at shoulder level. You turn the rope around the roller until the weight comes all the way up to your chest level. Use a reverse motion to unroll the rope and take the rope back to its starting position.

Step-By-Step Technique

You may not have a wrist roller, so let's start by making a homemade one. All you need is one of your gym plates, a strong rope and a bar. The plate can be a 5 or 10 pound weight plate, the rope should be strong and thin, about 3 feet long and a bar that's about 6 inches in diameter. Securely fasten the rope to the plate and tie the other end of the rope to the bar.
Stand straight, with your back upright and your chest sticking out a little – this helps you to be more stable. Your feet should be about a foot apart.
Grab your wrist roller (a normal grip with palms facing downwards will do) and start to rapidly roll the rope around the bar. This will lift the weight up and

up towards your chest. Your arms should remain straight and parallel to the floor all this time and your grip should be about shoulder width.

Once you have rolled all the rope, you will have your plate in front of your chest. Hold it there for a while, tighten your muscles and feel them contract.

Then with the opposite motion, slowly unroll the rope so that the plate goes back down to its original position. As your plate rolls up and down, it should be directly parallel with you, which means that your arms must be stretched out straight. You'll feel your muscles relax as the weight goes down, but not completely.

Repeat using your normal rep cycle, or as many times as you can. As you do your reps, your arms should not move from their original position.

Dealing with Injury

The most common injury here is to the wrist – you can easily break or bruise the wrist flexors. If you take on a weight that's too heavy to start with, you also risk tearing a muscle in your forearm, bicep or even shoulder.

To avoid injury, make sure to follow instructions. Get your muscles warmed up before you start the exercise. Also start with a light plate and as you get the arm muscles more into form, you can increase the weight.

As the wrists are sensitive, if you feel and abrasion or tenderness, it's best to stop. If it is bad, see a doctor. Forearm muscles heal pretty fast on their own, and if you hurt yourself, all you have to do is give that part of your body a rest from exercise for a while.

Variations

Tie the rope to a dumbbell or a barbell instead of a plate. Be careful with these though, they are very likely to swing towards your shins and could hurt you.

To put variations of stress on the muscles, you can vary the diameter of your grip bar – make it bigger or slightly smaller.

You can try to do the exercise with your legs a little farther apart to place different stress on the muscles. Not too far apart though, or you will lose balance.

Training Tips & Secrets

As with any other upper body exercise, keep increasing the weight that you lift gradually.

The bar may be hard to grip and may keep slipping – have some chalk with you.

Remember to rapidly raise the plate and then slowly drop it. Raising it slowly is almost ineffective.

You can vary the rapidity with which you raise the plate and drop it.

Reverse Dumbbell Curls

Introduction & Description

You are still working on those forearms and biceps, and want to try something different. Why don't you try the reverse dumbbell curl? By this stage of your training, you have probably come across the dumbbell curl, so this is just the dumbbell curl in reverse. It aims at two sets of muscles, primarily the outer forearms and secondarily, the biceps. Additionally, as you get to the height of your lift, your wrist muscles also come into play, which is a plus. To grip the dumbbells, your palms will face outwards towards the floor as opposed to upwards in a normal dumbbell curl. And the great thing is, you can do them while sitting or standing!

Anatomy & Biomechanics

Reverse dumbbell curls work on specific forearm and bicep muscles - brachialis and brachioradialis. Which muscle you work depends on whether you do the exercise while sitting down or standing. If you stand, you will work on both the biceps and the forearms, whilst if you sit, you will work more on the forearms. It's really up to you, but I would recommend that you try out both techniques during your sessions. It is an isolation exercise (works on an isolated set of muscles), so you need to make sure that you do other arm exercises to get an all-rounded workout.

Step-By-Step Technique

Since we can do this both sitting and standing, I'll describe separately how you do both:

Standing:

Here's where we work both the forearms and the biceps. Use the following steps.

Stand with your feet firmly planted on the ground, about a foot apart. Your body should be aligned, your back straight and your chest sticking out slightly. Your arms will be in by your sides.

With palms facing downwards and away from you (towards the floor), grasp your dumbbells. Your thumbs should be in the normal position – it's more comfortable.

Slowly raise the dumbbells to chest level. As you do this, your elbows remain firmly by your sides. Keep lifting until your arms are perpendicular to the floor. You will feel especially your bicep muscles tightening.

Once you have your dumbbells at the chest level, stop for a second and squeeze your forearm and bicep muscles.

Slowly lower the dumbbells to your starting position – you will feel your muscles relax but do not let them completely go. Keep them just a little contracted.

Repeat using your normal rep cycle or as many times as you can.

Sitting:

This one targets the forearm more:

Sit on a flat bench and rest your forearms on your thighs. Make sure to have your feet firmly planted on the ground and your buttocks resting comfortably on the bench.

Lean forward so that your fingers are dangling over your knees and your palms are facing outwards and towards the floor.

Grasp you dumbbells. For this too, just use a normal grasp.

Slowly raise the dumbbells to chin level. As you do this, your elbows remain firmly on your thighs. Keep lifting until your arms are perpendicular to the floor. You will feel your bicep muscles tightening.

At the highest point, stop for a few seconds, tightening your forearm and bicep muscles as you do so.

Slowly bring the dumbbells back down to their original position. If you do this correctly, you will feel your forearm muscles stretch, but not completely relax. They should still remain a little contracted.

Repeat using your normal rep cycle, or as many times as you can.

Dealing with Injury

In this exercise, you are most likely to tear muscles in your forearm or your bicep. Be careful – this can put you out of upper body exercise for quite a while. The commonest injuries are to the elbows and to the specific muscles in the biceps and forearms – the brachialis, brachioradialis and pronator teres. As you bring the weights down, you may over-extend your arm and overstrain your elbows. This can lead to biceps tendonitis or anterior capsule strain. These are just complex names for muscle abrasions or tears in the biceps. Remember the muscles involved in this exercise are pretty small and this makes them susceptible to injury if not handled carefully.

As with any exercise routine, make sure that you follow instructions. If you hurt yourself, take a break from exercising that particular set of muscles for some time. Depending on how bad it is, seek medical advice. The good thing is though, that biceps heal pretty quickly.

Variations

You can start the exercise with one arm, and then alternate. Keep switching but make sure that the reps are equal on each arm so that you get a balanced stretch on both sides.

You can use a normal grip – palms facing inwards and towards you. The initial time you tried it, your palms were facing outwards. Now try grasping your weights with your palms facing inwards towards your face.

Instead of dumbbells try a barbell. It will work just as well, although the flexibility may be more reduced than when using the dumbbells.

You can make variations on the speed at which you raise and lower the weights; you can try 2 or 3 different speeds within the same session. Control your speed though – if you do it too fast you may end up injuring yourself.

Training Tips & Secrets

Whether you are sitting or standing, make sure that throughout, your back remains straight. Your forearms and biceps will end up doing all the lifting and getting that much better.

Put a thrust into your initial lift, but make sure to lower the weight slowly to avoid over-extending your elbows.

Keep building muscle and strength by increasing the weight that you lift, but this must be done gradually. A sudden increase in weight is one of the quickest ways to get a torn muscle or a sprained wrist.

Your elbows will move around quite a bit during this exercise - keep your joints well lubricated by eating the right food such as Omega 3.

Reverse Cable Curl

Introduction & Description

This exercise focuses on working the forearms using a straight bar. It's called "reverse" because the palms, instead of facing upwards, towards you, face downwards towards the floor. The stress is mainly on the upper, outer forearm. The reverse cable curl is very similar to a dumbbell or barbell curl, the only difference being that the grasp is reversed, and that this one requires that you specifically use a straight bar or a cable.

Anatomy & Biomechanics

The upper outer forearm, or brachioradialis, is the main muscle that gets worked in this exercise. This is the muscle that helps to flex your forearm backwards and forwards at the elbow. In fact, it's jokingly called the beer-drinkers muscle, as it's the main muscle that's used when you raise your beer glass to your mouth and back down onto the counter.

As you lift and lower the cable during the exercise, this muscle will contract and relax and eventually become bigger and stronger. It's an important muscle to build if you are looking for upper body strength, because if it's strong enough, other lifting should be that much more fun for you!

Step-By-Step Technique

Stand straight with your feet firmly planted on the floor. They should be at least a foot apart.

Make sure that your back is straight.

Your palms should face downwards, away from you and towards the floor. Grasp the bar and using your forearm muscles, raise it slowly towards your chest, and stop just below your chin. As you grasp, your thumbs should be in the normal position i.e. they do not have to go under and around the bar.

All this while, your upper arms and elbows should be tightly pressed close to your body. It's tempting to get your upper arms or shoulders in to help, but remember only your forearms should do the lifting.

When you get the bar to your chin level, pause for a second and squeeze your forearm muscles. If you grasped your bar properly, your palms will now be facing outwards, away from your chest.

Using some resistance, slowly lower the bar back to its starting point, somewhere midway of your thighs.

Dealing with Injury

The most common injuries are to the elbows and to the specific muscles in the biceps – the brachioradialis or even the brachialis. You may bring the cable down too fast and end up tearing a muscle or a ligament. Worse still, bringing the cable down too fast may jerk your elbows and leave you with both elbow joint and muscle injuries. Remember the muscles involved in this exercise are pretty small and this makes them susceptible to injury if not handled carefully.

As with any exercise routine, make sure that you follow instructions.

Remember to warm up before you get started. The exercise has several variations, but make sure that your muscles are primed before you try any of them.

If you hurt yourself, take a break from exercising that particular set of muscles for some time. Of course, if you feel it's serious, seek medical advice. The good thing is though, that biceps heal pretty quickly.

Variations

Variations are really a way to do the same exercise but target the same muscles from different angles. They also put more fun into your training. There can be several variations of the reverse cable curl:

You can do a one arm reverse cable curls. For this you will use a dumbbell and alternately exercise the arms. Follow the instructions as you would if you were using two arms. Make sure that you do equal reps for each arm.

You can opt to use dumbbells instead, to get more flexibility into your lifting. Dumbbells are harder to control during your lift though, so you have to be extra cautious with these.

You can also opt to use a barbell. In fact, you can start easy without the plates at the end , and eventually add the plates for more stress on the forearms.

You can place your cable on a bench, and instead of starting your lift at your thighs, you could start your lift from the bench.

Training Tips & Secrets

Lean slightly forward throughout your movement. The temptation may be to lean back, but leaning forwards benefits your forearm muscles more.

You might find that you rock on your feet as you lift – try not to do this. The more stable you are, the more your forearms are doping the heavy lifting.

Try different widths in your grip – tickle those hard-to-reach muscles! Make the grips narrower or wider.

For the narrower width, use a lighter weight.

Dead lift

The dead lift is a classic grip training exercise. Not only grip but also overall body strength is developed. Many athletes use wrist straps to make the move easier but we want to make it harder. To do this a thicker than normal barbell is used and no straps.

Popular variations of the dead lift include stiff legged, sumo and alternating grip. There are many others. Along with squat and bench press this is a core power exercise. A similar effect for the hands and forearms can be achieved with weighted pull-ups. This is equally taxing on the arms but not so much elsewhere like the lower body.

ADDITIONAL TRAINING

There are literally hundreds of grip exercises that can be performed with everyday equipment. I can't list them all here and there is little point when the best of them are described in depth in John Brookfield's two great books.

Some other grip training methods include:

Gripping a door and leaning back with your body weight.
Lifting a chair from a single leg with one hand.
Tearing phone books and card packs.
Screwing up newspapers and towels on a single hand.
Carrying heavy buckets and weights over distance in your hands.
Lifting heavy boulders and rocks.
Nail and rebar bending.
Power twister training.

Gymnastic ring training.
Breaking matches between the fingers.
Bending beer bottle tops.
Crushing apples and soda cans.
Brick lifting.
Weighted Pull-ups.
Farmers Walk.
Fingertip pushups.
Twisting and cutting steel wire with pliers.
Rope Climbing & Tug-O-War
Hand & Finger Dexterity Training

During the course of Iron Palm and hard gong training your hands and joints will come under greater than normal stress. It is important to perform remedial exercises to enhance the health of the joints and maintain superior dexterity.

Rather than repeat another person's work I will refer you to a very good book called "Finger Fitness – the art of finger control". The book provides a very in-depth finger manipulation program that will maintain your dexterity. This is the best program of its kind.

You also want to invest in some inexpensive Chinese Balls and embark on enhancing your dexterity and endurance with these also.

Tui Na Hand and Arm Massage

Hand massage is an essential component to Iron Palm. Without the massage you are only doing half the training and may eventually experience damage. When you use the Dit Da Jow you are to rigorously massage it into the hands for a prolonged period of time. Do not just soak the hands or briefly massage them.

As for the methods of massage I have mentioned the wall bag video from the UK Wing Chun association. This covers hand massage for martial artists. James Sinclair's Master's Class DVD from the same place also covers hand massage. There are also books specifically on the subject. Mantak Chia has a Chi Kung massage book called "Chi Self Massage" and there are numerous books on reflexology but really the Wing Chun DVD's are highly recommended. The only fault is that he does not use enough Jow.

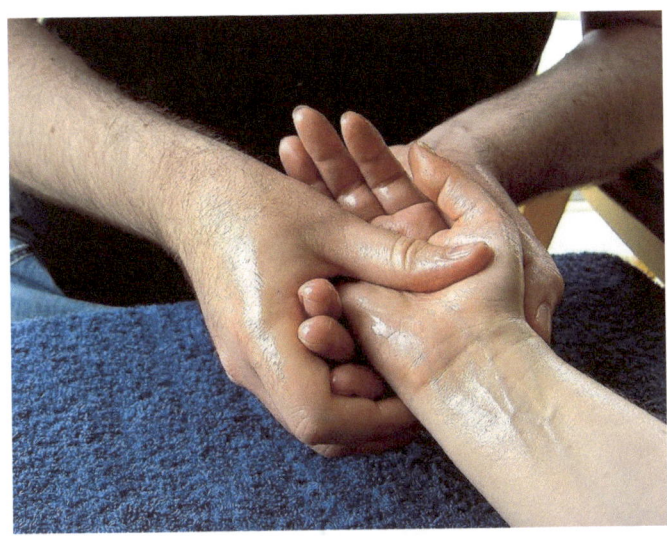

creative commons copyright, Attribute Lubyanka

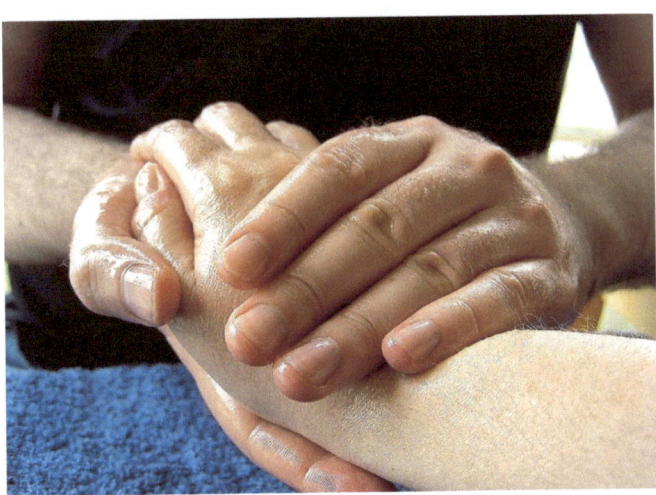

creative commons copyright, Attribute Lubyanka

In this section we will briefly examine some self massage you can perform to compliment your Iron Palm and Iron Arm conditioning. First there is a section on general arm, hand and shoulder massage. We will also discuss "tennis elbow" and "carpal tunnel" as these are common injuries for athletes concentrating on grip and forearm strength. As always you must use Dit Da Jow liniment liberally while massaging.

Arm & Hand Massage

Massage with the thumbs and fingers the acupuncture points as illustrated below.

1. Jian Nei Shu

2. Jian Yu

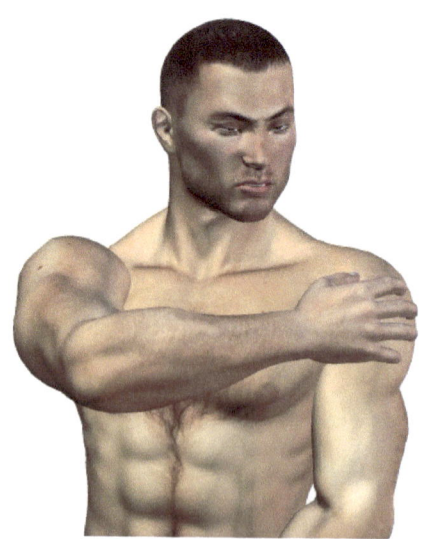

3. Jian Jing

4. Qu Chi

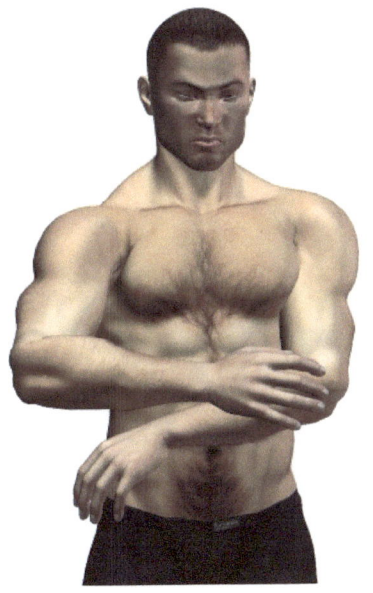

5. Xiao Hai

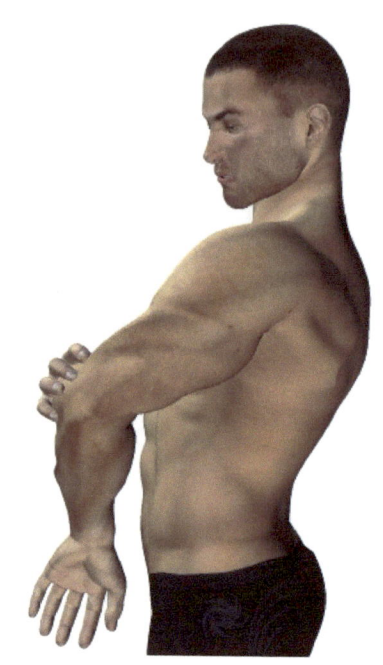

6. Shou San Li

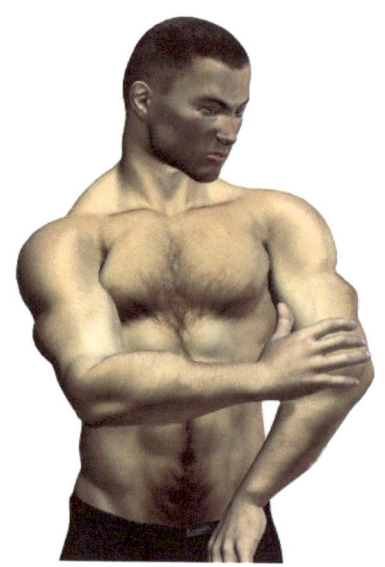

7. Yang Chi

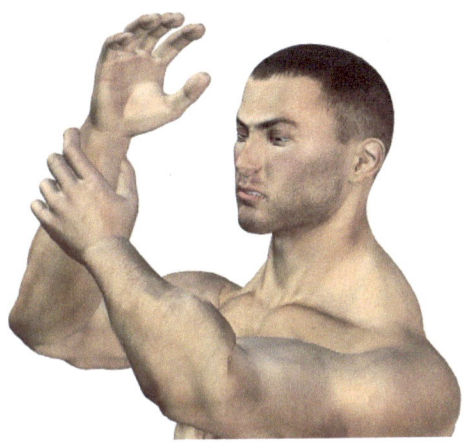

8. He Gu

(Meaty part of hand between thumb and fore finger)

Squeezing and massaging the arm.

Relax the arm and improve circulation by kneading up and down the muscles several times.

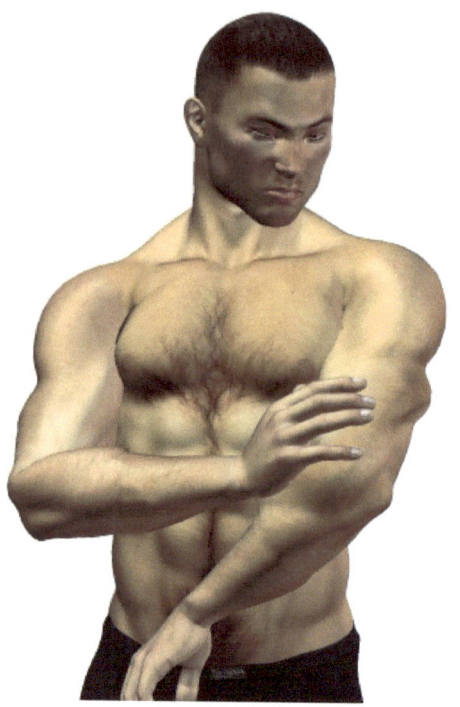

Rub up and down the inside and side of the arms 20-30 times on each arm.

Very gently twist and pull each finger and thumb on both hands.

Rub the palms and back of the hands.

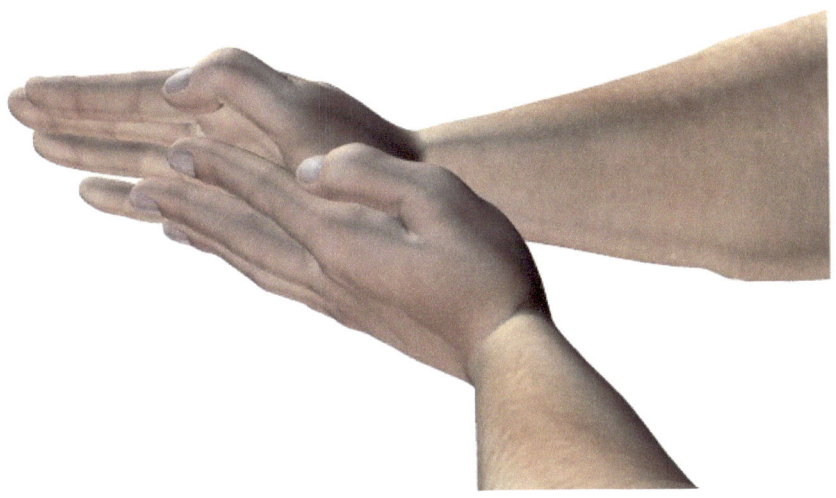

Knead the palm, fingers, base of the thumb and back of the hand deeply with Dit Da Jow for 20 – 30 minutes.

Grab at the air and employ tension while extending the forearms then relax and draw the hands toward the body. Repeat several times.

Tennis Elbow Treatment

Tennis elbow is quite a common injury for Iron Palm students. Pain is felt on the outside of the elbow joint usually when muscle force is exerted. If it appears on the inside of the elbow it is known as golfers elbow.

1. Press and massage the outside of the elbow, forearm and wrist.

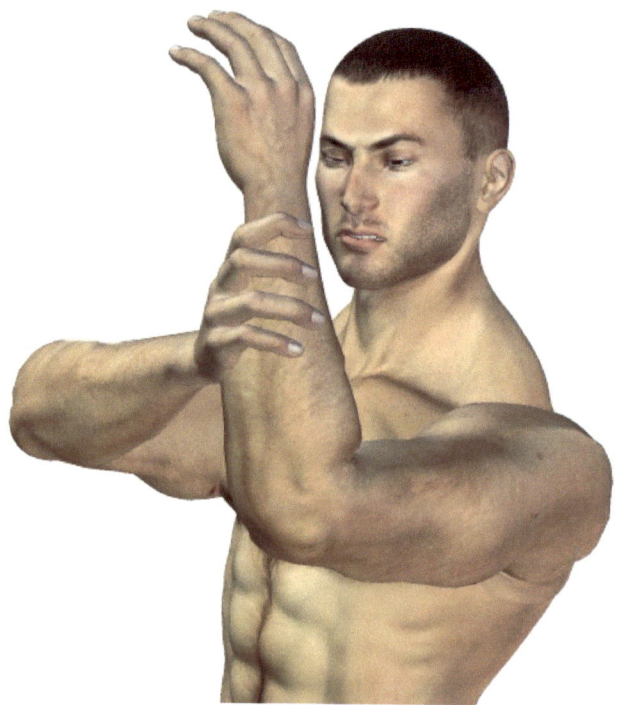

2. Massage the acupuncture meridians on the outside of the arm. Qu chi and Shou san li points should be massaged.

3. Find the tender points with the most pain and knead these with the thumb.

4. Flex and rotate the elbows.

5. Rub the affected part of the elbow so you feel heat.

Carpal Tunnel Treatment

Carpal Tunnel is a sheath of fascia surrounding the nerves to the hand that is found in the wrist. When this sheath is damaged the nerves can become inflamed causing pain and paralysis. Carpal tunnel syndrome is very common.

Massage when combined with remedial exercise can cure the condition.

Massage Treatment.

1. Press the underside of the affected arm.

2. Press acupuncture points on the arm 100 times.

    Qu ze

    Nei Guan

    Yu ji

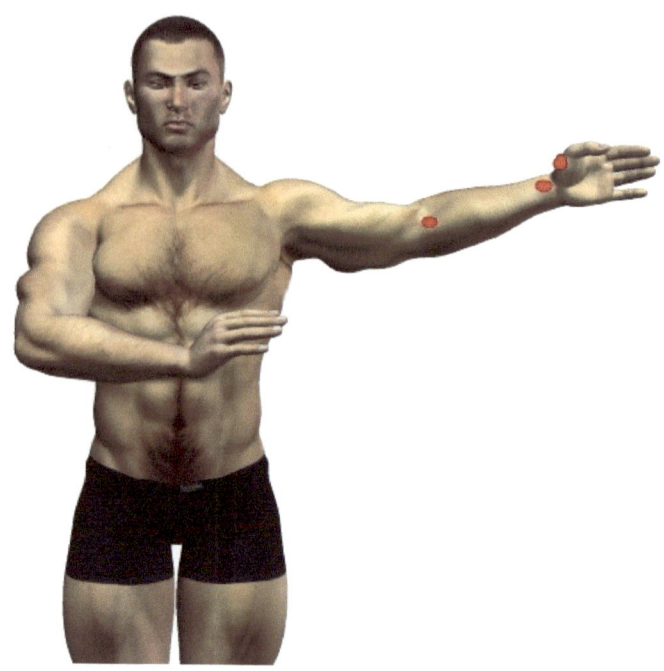

3. Massage the carpal tunnel in the affected arm for several minutes.

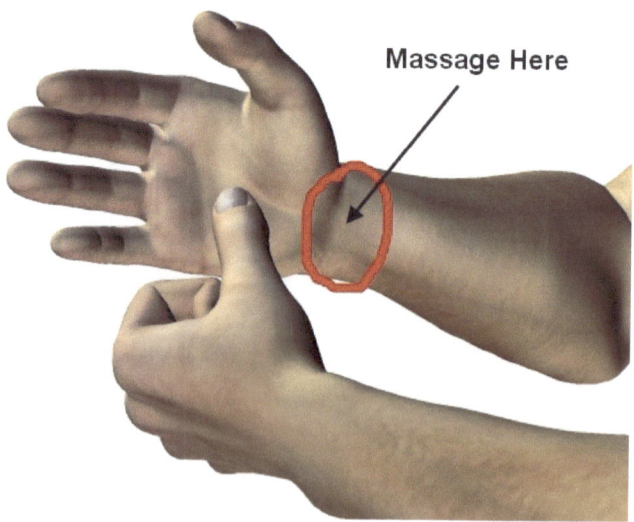

4. Gently rotate the wrist in both directions

5. Rub the underside of the palm and forearm from the elbow toward the hand.

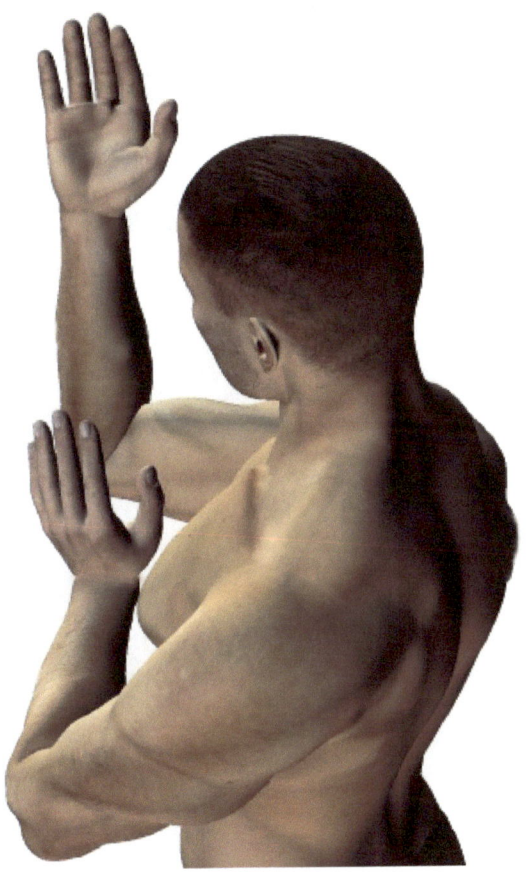

Remedial exercises:

The following exercises can help to cure both carpal tunnel and tennis elbow. They can also be used preventatively while developing grip strength.

1. Hold a sheet of newspaper in a single hand and screw the paper up into a tight ball without assistance from the other hand. Repeat for an even number of times in each hand until you are unable to do more.

2. Grab at the air and employ tension while extending the forearms then relax and draw the hands toward the body. Repeat several times.

3. Wring out a soaked towel into a bucket of water until the towel is dry.

4. Flex and relax the wrist and forearm as illustrated below.

SAMPLE ROUTINES FOR IRON QIGONG & STRENGTH TRAINING

Let us begin with a basic program for a person with minimal time.

Assuming that you perform regular weight training, cardio and stretching which you should be doing in addition to your Qi Gong.

A minimum of 30 minutes per day is required to develop Iron Palm. As this exercise is neither aerobic nor anaerobic it will not result in over training if done along with other exercise.

Use the Flat Bag initially filled with hard, dry beans. Strike using the multiple hand positions as instructed. Don't bother to count repetitions just stick to the duration of 30 minutes. Following this massage with Dit Da Jow for 15-20 minutes. You can massage & apply Jow prior to and during the training as you please.

If you have an hour to spare you can add Iron Arm conditioning also following the same principles.

After 3 months change to a bag of small stones, after another 3 months steel shot (shotgun pellets) and finally after another 3 months steel ball bearings.

Once this level is reached you will not revert to anything less that steel ball bearings but you may if you desire train on solid steel and concrete. Always use Jow.

In the second year you could if you wish add a second session per day or preferably you could make your "bamboo leaf hand" hanging bag and use that.

The point is that you can begin "bamboo leaf hand" at any time you desire. But the filling should be the same as your Iron Palm flat bag. This is why it is preferable to keep your Iron Palm and Iron Arm at the same level of development. So you can train on the same bag fillings for various exercises. If one lags more bruising will occur for a time.

So in year two add another Iron Palm session or begin Bamboo Leaf Hand also.

At this point your training would consist of 30 minutes Iron Palm, 30 minutes Iron Arm and minimum 30 minutes "bamboo leaf hand".

On top of this if you have the time you can also do Iron body conditioning. Doing all of these methods could take 2-3 hours per day quite easily.

This is a big time commitment but 30-60 minutes of relaxing Iron Palm / Iron Arm is achievable by everybody.

Following this after a year of each you should be able to tolerate beating with steel and feel no pain or discomfort from this. The final progression then is to add weight to your bamboo leaf hand hanging bag, 10 kg every 3 months and to your Iron Arm roller.

Eventually you will have a 200 – 300 lb hanging bag filled with ball bearings and a solid steel Iron Arm roller. Your flat bag will also be filled with steel ball bearings.

Once this level is reached in 2-3 years you really don't need to add to the hard gong training but should be mastering internal methods in addition.

The ultimate goal is to be a master of internal & external, hard & soft. We do not cover internal Iron Palm in Iron Power Palm but sources of information have been provided.

A realistic time frame if you train diligently everyday is five years to master both internal and external methods.

Muscular strength routines for the hands and forearms follow. These are more regimented.

Example Super Gripper program:

Week : 1

1, 5, 9 (195.6) x 8 _ _ _ _ _ _ _ _ _ _ _ _ _ _ _
2, 5, 10 (225.5) x 5 _ _ _ _ _ _ _ _ _ _ _ _ _ _
2, 6, 10 (240.4) x 3 _ _ _ _ _ _ _ _ _ _ _ _ _ _
1, 6, 11 (256.2) x 3 _ _ _ _ _ _ _ _ _ _ _ _ _ _

2, 4, 12 (261.4) x 3 _ _ _ _ _ _ _ _ _ _ _ _ _ _

Week : 2

    1, 5, 9 (195.6) x 8 _ _ _ _ _ _ _ _ _ _ _ _ _ _
    2, 5, 10 (225.5) x 5 _ _ _ _ _ _ _ _ _ _ _ _ _
    1, 7, 10 (249.2) x 3 _ _ _ _ _ _ _ _ _ _ _ _ _
    2, 4, 12 (261.4) x 3 _ _ _ _ _ _ _ _ _ _ _ _ _
    2, 6, 11 (264.1) x 3 _ _ _ _ _ _ _ _ _ _ _ _ _

Week : 3

    1, 5, 9 (195.6) x 8 _ _ _ _ _ _ _ _ _ _ _ _ _ _
    1, 4, 11 (228.1) x 5 _ _ _ _ _ _ _ _ _ _ _ _ _
    2, 4, 12 (261.4) x 3 _ _ _ _ _ _ _ _ _ _ _ _ _
    1, 7, 11 (272.9) x 3 _ _ _ _ _ _ _ _ _ _ _ _ _

Week : 4

    1, 5, 9 (195.6) x 8 _ _ _ _ _ _ _ _ _ _ _ _ _ _
    1, 6, 10 (232.5) x 5 _ _ _ _ _ _ _ _ _ _ _ _ _
    8, 11 (277.6) x 3 _ _ _ _ _ _ _ _ _ _ _ _ _

Week : 5

    2, 6, 8 (198.3) x 8 _ _ _ _ _ _ _ _ _ _ _ _ _ _
    1, 6, 10 (232.5) x 5 _ _ _ _ _ _ _ _ _ _ _ _ _
    2, 6, 11 (264.1) x 3 _ _ _ _ _ _ _ _ _ _ _ _ _
    1, 7, 11 (272.9) x 3 _ _ _ _ _ _ _ _ _ _ _ _ _
    2, 7, 11 (280.8) x 3 _ _ _ _ _ _ _ _ _ _ _ _ _

Week : 6

    2, 6, 8 (198.3) x 8 _ _ _ _ _ _ _ _ _ _ _ _ _ _
    1, 6, 10 (232.5) x 5 _ _ _ _ _ _ _ _ _ _ _ _ _
    1, 8, 10 (267.6) x 3 _ _ _ _ _ _ _ _ _ _ _ _ _
    3, 6, 11 (273.8) x 3 _ _ _ _ _ _ _ _ _ _ _ _ _

3, 5, 12 (284.3) x 3 _____

Week : 7

3, 11 (203.0) x 8 _____
2, 7, 9 (235.1) x 5 _____
8, 11 (277.6) x 3 _____
2, 6, 12 (289.5) x 3 _____

Week : 8

3, 11 (203.0) x 8 _____
3, 7, 9 (244.8) x 5 _____
4, 8, 10 (296.6) x 3

This is generated with the super gripper software and the target is a 300 lb grip.

The first 3 numbers show spring positions, then the resistance in pounds then the number of reps. You should be training 3-5 days per week. If you don't have a super gripper then individual grippers roughly matching the resistances would be substituted.

The super gripper software can spit out unlimited custom programs.

Single torsion hand gripper workouts:

Regular grippers can be used with the spring pointing upward or inverted with in pointing to the ground. Both positions should be trained.

Using the other hand to assist positioning the gripper is called "setting". To develop maximum strength you want to minimize this unless doing negatives.

Beginners should train with grippers 2-3 times per week but with experience this can be increased.

Specific routines depend upon your maximum resistance level.

First you want to do 6 – 10 reps on an easy gripper such as the 100 lb. I also warm-up on a rubber donut which is about 70 lbs. Do your warm-ups inverted also.

Then move up to something slightly harder and do 3 - 4 crushes.

Use your goal gripper for 4 squeezes each hand. Then 4 negative squeezes,

Move up to a harder gripper and now do your negatives with the other hand assisting to close then resist the gripper opening with one hand alone. 3 negatives each hand.

We discussed negative reps in the strength training principles section. In addition to negatives you can make a choker to keep the handles within the most difficult range.

Advanced trainees can do double to triple the number of repetitions. This is pretty tough but the KTA program uses vastly more reps and is done 6 days per week.

You must also do 3 - 4 sets of 4 reps with a thumb clamp (spring clamp) each workout to strengthen your thumbs.

Also do work on the extensors with elastic bands or by opening the hands in the steel shot bucket.

Other grip methods can be used as supplementary training.

Barbell and Dumbbell Routines:

Beginner:

    Workout 1
    Reverse wrist curl   1 – 3 sets   7 - 12 reps

Wrist curl   1 – 3 sets   7 - 12 reps
Workout 2
Wrist Roller 3 sets   7 – 12 reps

Intermediate Routines:

Workout 1
Barbell Preacher Reverse Curls   3 sets   7-12 reps
Dumbbell Wrist Curls   3 sets   10 -14 reps
Barbell Reverse Wrist Curls   3 sets   10 -14 reps
workout 2
Zottman Curls   3 sets   12 -15 reps
Reverse Barbell Curls   3 sets   12 -15 reps
Wrist Curls   3 sets   12 -15 reps

Advanced Routines:

Workout 1
Hammer Curls   4 sets 7 -12 reps
Barbell reverse Wrist Curls   4 sets   10-15 reps
Cable Reverse Wrist Curls   4 sets   10-15 reps
Workout 2
Seat Barbell Wrist Curls
   (Palms facing upwards)   3 sets 7 – 12 reps
Wrist Curls Over A Bench
   (Palms facing downwards)   3 sets 7 – 12 reps
Reverse Cable Curls   3 sets 7 – 12 reps

Resources

Iron Palm:

Books and Videos

www.IronPalm.com
www.ukwingchun.com/
www.clearsilat.com/
www.universal-tao.com/
www.briangray.com/
www.wle.com/

Dit Da Jow

www.Ebay.com
www.Amazon.com
www.IronPalm.com
www.TheIronlotusSociety.com
www.seaofchi.com/tlu.html
www.plumdragonherbs.com
www.scarfamilyditdajow.com
www.shenmartialarts.com
www.coilingdragon.com
ww.eastearthtrade.com
www.orientalherb.com

Equipment

www.ebay.com
www.amazon.com
www.wle.com
www.sakuramartialarts.com
www.everythingwingchun.com

Information

www.ironpalm.com

Grip Strength Training:

Books and Videos

www.samsonscroll.com/
www.atomicathletic.com

Equipment

www.samsonscroll.com/
www.ironmind.com/
www.atomicathletic.com
www.slatershardware.com

Information

www.gripboard.com
www.ultimategripstrength.com
www.functionalhandstrength.com/

After Word

I hope you enjoy this book as much as I have enjoyed researching and compiling it. Certainly you must begin your Iron Palm program immediately. Buy or make a bag, get some Jow and begin. The reward is great and the effort small.

Few people have the knowledge to become an Iron Palm. You now have the knowledge.

Use your new skill with modesty and discretion for self defence only.

www.ingramcontent.com/pod-product-compliance
Lightning Source LLC
Chambersburg PA
CBHW042055290426
44111CB00001B/9